6.56

THEOLOGICAL MODELS FOR THE PARISH

THEOLOGICAL MODELS FOR THE PARISH

SABBAS J. KILIAN, OFM

ALBA · HOUSE NEW · YORK

SOCIETY OF ST. PAUL, 2187 VICTORY BLVD., STATEN ISLAND, NEW YORK 10314

Library of Congress Cataloging in Publication Data

Kilian, Sabbas, 1916-
   Theological models for the parish.

   Includes bibliographical references.
   1. Parishes. 2. Church. I. Title.
BX1746.K49 1977   262'.22   76-42986
ISBN 0-8189-0337-6

Nihil Obstat:
Joseph P. Penna, J.C.D.
Censor Librorum

Imprimatur:
✠ *James P. Mahoney, D.D.*
Vicar General, Archdiocese of New York
September 20, 1976

The Nihil Obstat and Imprimatur
are a declaration that a book or pamphlet is considered
to be free from doctrinal or moral error. It is not implied that
those who have granted the Nihil Obstat and Imprimatur agree
with the contents, opinions or statements expressed.

Designed, printed and bound in the United States of
America by the Fathers and Brothers of the Society of St. Paul,
2187 Victory Boulevard, Staten Island, New York, 10314,
as part of their communications apostolate.

2 3 4 5 6 7 8 9 (Current Printing: first digit).

PREFACE

Most of my twenty-six years in the United States of America have been spent in New York or the New York metropolitan area. Nine of those years were entirely devoted to pastoral life in the national parish of St. Stephen of Hungary, New York City, and to its weekly radio-program, "The Voice of Faith." As I moved into teaching, I always felt that contact with the community of believers was important for me. How could I teach ecclesiology without actually experiencing the realization of the universal Church in its most concrete local expression, the parish?

Therefore, I continued serving parishes throughout my life in America. Six years ago, I moved to St. Ursula's Parish, and my experiences there have contributed, in no small measure, to the maturing of my thoughts on the parish. I hope that they can be of some help to all those who are interested in the theology of the parish.

I am tremendously grateful to the people of St. Ursula's Parish, especially to the members of the Discussion Club and the Prayer Group, for allowing me to work with them for God's kingdom. I also readily acknowledge my indebtedness to my students at Fordham University and those of the Institute in Pastoral Ministry of St. Joseph College, West Hartford, Connecticut, whose challenges only stimulated me to more research and reflection.

Katie LaCugna, a graduate student, and Dr. Patrick Carey, a former student of mine, together with my many friends who have always encouraged me in my work have earned my eternal gratitude and thanks. And finally, my most appreciative expression of thanks should go to Anthony Buono who edited my manuscript and to his dear wife, Margaret, who did such a splendid job in typing it. Faithful friends as they are, they have been most helpful and co-operative in giving final form to this manuscript.

Sabbas J. Kilian, O.F.M.

INTRODUCTION

The parish is a vital and important part of Christian life. It fully displays the Christian life's sacramental and communal dimensions. The study of the nature and structure of the parish should, therefore, be of fundamental interest not only to pastors, priests, and parishioners, but also to theologians. Unfortunately, pastoral theology has not yet gained equal status with the other disciplines of Roman Catholic theology, and consequently it has not been cultivated, apart from the training of future priests, as an integral branch of the whole theological enterprise. As a matter of fact, until recently theologians spent little time studying the complex nature of the parish. They left such studies either to canon lawyers or sociologists. Recent developments in the theological outlook, especially from the viewpoint of ecclesiology, coupled with genuine efforts toward theological and ecclesial renewal, have brought about a better understanding of the parish and of pastoral theology in general, and inspired even theologians to devote their research and reflection to the theological reality of the parish.

In this study, we theologically analyze the parish to determine its scope, significance and methodology. We intend to deal with five possible theological models, rooted in the nature of both the Church and the parish, and proposed here as facilitators of the contemporary approach to the parish. In this context, the following topics are developed:

1) A short history of the parish.
2) The theological elements of the notion of the Church and the parish.
3) Theological models of the parish:
   a) A community gathered together to hear the word of God.
   b) A community gathered together to celebrate the Eucharist.
   c) A local organization of the universal Church.
   d) A community restructured into small subcommunities.
   e) The American parish: the agent of change.

It is hoped that by studying these particular aspects of the parish, a very valuable contribution can be made toward a clearer understanding of both its nature and its proper function in our contemporary society.

CONTENTS

THEOLOGICAL MODELS FOR THE PARISH

CHAPTER I

THE PARISH IN HISTORY

From the Beginnings to Trent

The parish, as it is known today, is not a biblical datum but a product of history. As such, the parish can grow and develop or deteriorate and even die. Nothing is permanent about it except its theological finality.[1]

Some historical research has claimed that the parish-system began to develop very early in the Church both in the cities and country. There were town-parishes, run by priests or deacons, in Gaul, "titular churches" in Rome and Antioch, and rural churches, first in Gaul from the fourth century, then in the typically rural setup of the Germanic peoples from the fifth and sixth centuries on. Though these all were forerunners of parish structures, they were not full-fledged parishes. Either they were still integral parts of the bishop's city-parish, consequently their pastors' powers were greatly restricted by the bishop, or interference on the part of the nobles who usually owned the churches hindered both the appointment of the local priest by and his ecclesial relationship with the bishop.

Furthermore, in the very early centuries, *local church, parish, diocese,* and *parochia* usually all referred to a local community under the more or less direct spiritual leadership of the bishop.[2] Whether one follows the Jerusalem or the Pauline line in establishing the structure of the early local churches, starting with the second century, the unique role of the bishop in the life of the local community cannot be questioned. He was the pastor of all the Christians living in or around his city. He was the celebrant of the Eucharist, the ordinary minister of the other sacraments, particularly baptism, and the preacher of the Word of God. Even while in prison, during the persecutions, he was the pastor of his flock though he delegated the exercise of some of his powers to one of his priests.

This prominence of the bishop in the proper functioning of the local community explains the presence of the country-bishops in North Africa in the fourth and fifth centuries, and of the *chorepiscopi* in the East from the third century on.[3] These institutions developed as efforts toward solving the growing problem of evangelizing the countryside, especially in the fourth century when the freedom granted to the Church made possible and viable such a massive program. The multiplication of country-bishops and *chorepiscopi*, however, was not the answer to the problem. Together with the country-churches in Gaul, and the titular churches of Rome and Antioch and the private churches (*Ecclesiae Propriae, Eigenkirche*) in Germany[4], the country bishops and *chorepiscopi* indicated that placeness belonged to the very nature of the local communities and required that the sacramental operations of the Church be defined and carried out accordingly. Yet it took a long time for the Church to discard many abortive initiatives and set the right path for further developments.[5]

Actually, this took place in the tenth and eleventh centuries, when, for the first time, we find several parishes in the same city. Such a development brought about an interesting ecclesial trend. On the one hand, the pastors of parish churches became more and more independent of the bishop of the territory, and also more and more canonical in their dealings with the people; on the other hand, the bishop ceased to be the pastor of the city parish and became the head if all the pastors under his jurisdiction. As canon law gained prominence in the West, pastor-faithful and bishop-pastors relationships got caught in the intricacies of man-made laws and their canonical interpretation. The theology that in times past had motivated interest in developing the parish-structure disappeared. Its absence, a poorly educated clergy, and excessive interest in material gain created a situation that no canon law could salvage from bankruptcy.

> In brief, a profound rebellion was being forged from the thirteenth century on. Theological insecurity, religious indifference, and a deep feeling of discontent with the clergy were to explode as the Protestant Reformation. In the meantime, parish priests and religious orders went on arguing about who would collect the parish profits.[5]

The Council of Trent

The Council of Trent reacted to both the Reformation and the confusion created by it in Western Christianity. In order to assure renewal and reorganization of the Catholic Church, the fathers of the Council had to see to it that the centers of Christian life, immediately available to the faithful on the local level, be able to function properly and effectively. Consequently,

> starting with the Council of Trent, the parish took on a new pastoral clarity; upon it and the diocese rested the entire religious reform undertaken by the Council fathers. The parish unquestionably took on a juridical aspect which was needed, on the other hand, to clarify a confused state of affairs. Ever since then the word "parish" has meant a clearly defined territory forming part of a diocese; this concept was later to pass intact into the Code of Canon Law.[7]

Here is the main text of the Council of Trent responsible for the canonical clarification of the parish.[8]

> ... In those cities and localities where the parochial churches have no definite boundaries, and whose rectors have not their own people whom they may rule but administer the sacraments indiscriminately to all who desire them, the holy council commands the bishops that, for the greater security of the salvation of the souls committed to them, they divide the people into definite and distinct parishes and assign to each its own and permanent parish priest, who can know his people and from whom alone they may licitly receive the sacraments; or that they make other, more beneficial provisions as the conditions of the locality may require. They shall also see to it that the same is done as soon as possible in those cities and localities where there are no parish churches; any privileges and customs whatsoever, even though immemorial, notwithstanding.[9]

This is the primary text responsible for the so-called "parochial principle" before the Code of Canon Law. The parochial principle embraces the parish principle by clearly ascribing the inhabitants of a defined territory to a parish within which they can partake of the sacraments; and also the parish-priest principle according to which only the parish priest of the locally determined parish can be the minister of the valid and licit administration of the sacraments. Interestingly enough, the reason given in the above text for establishing the parish principle is "the greater security of the salvation of the souls committed to" the bishops. Evidently, wherever the parochial principle had not been in use before the Council of Trent, the faithful must have encountered great difficulties in being provided with the sacraments. The root of the problem was twofold. Either no parish church was available to the faithful or no parish priest was permanently assigned to the parish with direct pastoral care for the parishioners. The above text was intended to solve both these problems by demanding precise territorial limits for each parish and by entrusting its permanent care to one priest-pastor with the provision that he reside in the parish, be bound to preach and to take care of the religious education of the youth.[10] It was established that, in cases of necessity, the bishops "compel the rectors, or those to whom it pertains, to associate with themselves in this office as many priests as are necessary to administer the sacraments and carry on divine worship."[11]

The Code of Canon Law

The Council of Trent, therefore, clearly established the parochial principle as a vitally important element in the life of the Church. Unfortunately, all this was done on a merely canonical basis. Theological considerations neither entered into the debate of the Council Fathers nor were they sought to justify the parochial principle. The situation has remained the same ever since, even after the promulgation of the Code. A quick look at the latter will verify this claim.

> The territory of every diocese is to be divided into distinct territorial parts; to each part is to be assigned its own church with a definite part of the population, and its own rector as the proper pastor of that territory is to be put in charge for the necessary care of souls (c. 216, no. 1).[12]

There is no fundamental difference between this text and that of the Council of Trent. However, the Code further clarifies the role of the rector by characterizing him as the "proper pastor" of the parish territory. Canon 451 is important in this regard. It describes the pastor as "a priest or moral person upon whom a parish is conferred in his own right (*in titulum*) with the care of souls to be exercised under the authority of the Ordinary of the place."[13] The proper and immediate spiritual care of the parishioners is then explicitly and directly entrusted to the pastor.

Although the Code did not abolish already existing personal (i.e., national parishes) and mixed parishes, (i.e., national and territorial), the future establishment of such new parishes is made dependent on special apostolic indult (c. 216, no. 4). This restriction seems to indicate that "the plain territorial parish is the preferred type because its government is less subject to confusion and difficulties."[14] And on this ground, one can conclude that, generally speaking, parish means, in the Code, a distinct, clearly limited territory and distinct, clearly determined population with its own proper church and its own proper pastor.[15] One can, therefore, say without exaggeration or distortion that the Code simply retained the parochial principle formulated by the Council of Trent by stressing both the parish-principle in its territorial setup and the parish-priest principle in the office of the pastor. The third element, the people of the parish, is referred to only indirectly, being the motivating element of the territorial division, but without becoming an essential part of the legal definition of the parish.

> This terminology of the Code reflects, as the Code does in many other respects, an inadequate ecclesiology, an ecclesiology that is one-sidedly clerical and concerned almost exclusively with hierarchical functions, and which does not give proper consideration to the community and to the functions of the laity.[16]

How true this is! Yet only in the first half of this twentieth century a great degree of uneasiness with the exclusively legalistic and overly clerical application of the parochial principle became detectable among laity, clergy, and theologians.[17] The voices of protest against a purely juridical approach to the parish have become throughout the century increasingly stronger. Sociologists of religion were the first to assert that community could not be established by setting up legal territorial parish boundaries. The sociologists also noticed from their studies that the Catholic's prime loyalty, as a Church member, no longer was to the parish.[18]

In light of these assertions of the sociologists, one could ask, "Has the parish had its day?"[19] If "parish" is defined simply canonically the answer could be "yes." However, if the parish is defined theologically and its proper functioning made clear, a real renaissance of the parish may take place. With accurate theological models to insure proper functioning, the parish can become the focal point of individual and communitarian growth in Christ. From a theological perspective,

> the mission of the parish can . . . pursue only one direction, and that is to bring all its subjects through all the various and graduated stages of development to their full maturity as persons made by a personal God and destined by Him to play an irreplaceable and unique role in the implementation of His plans for humanity.[20]

CHAPTER II

THEOLOGICAL ELEMENTS OF THE NOTION OF THE CHURCH AND THE PARISH

1. The Emergence of the Theological Notion of the Parish

In the brief review of the history of the parish no reference was made to the Second Vatican Council. The omission was intentional, not an oversight. Vatican II was not in line with the legalistic approach to the parish found in Trent and the Code. Unlike Trent or the Code, Vatican II presented *theological* insights about the nature of the Church; this resulted in valuable discoveries even about the nature of the parish. The Council, therefore, deserves special and careful analysis. Before analyzing these new insights of Vatican II, it is necessary, however, to examine the preconciliar developments that made possible this new theological and non-legalistic approach to the Church and parish.

We can pinpoint five major reasons for interest in the theological reflection on the parish in the years preceding Vatican II:[21]

1) The renewal of ecclesiology begun in the last century by Moehler, the Tubingen school, and Scheeben spread steadily after World War I and received official approbation in the encyclical *Mystici Corporis* of Pius XII. This laid stress on the concept of the Church as essentially mystical and supernatural rather than juridical and hierarchical,

leading to the conclusion that the supernatural aspect of the Church must be reflected in institutions such as the parish.

2) The liturgical movement officially begun by Pius X in his 1903 *Motu Proprio* had important repercussions. This movement's systematic study of the essence and history of the liturgy laid the basis for viewing the pastor and his functions—and hence the parish—as elements filled with a meaning that had been relegated to the background by the emphasis placed on the juridical aspect of the Church and of pastoral care. Specifically, the idea of the parish as the Eucharistic community fostered theological interest and research.

3) In Germany, the parish emerged as the sole Catholic organization or structured activity that was not or could not be prohibited by the Nazi regime. The fact that the parish alone succeeded in keeping the Church's life-line open during that period catapulted the parish back into the limelight and caused many theologians to take a second look at it.

4) A new pastoral theology emerged, turning from an empirical discipline of counseling methods and techniques for achieving a successful apostolate into a true theological science. This set the stage for the study of the pastoral aspect of the parish and for considering pastoral functions as supernatural activities, worthy of theological considerations. The logical corollary resulting therefrom was that the theological understanding of the Church's pastoral mission and work must oversee all empirical investigations.

5) Gabriel Le Bras' famous manifesto issued in 1931 inspired a host of socio-ecclesial studies of the parish and thus contributed to the continuing debate concerning its true aspect.

These and many other reasons certainly helped the parish gain the attention and excite the curiosity of theologians concerning the history and the true nature of the parish-system of the Church. As a result, several trends emerged in the last fifteen years before the Council. Some of them, as we shall see, postulated the need for a theology of the parish[22] while others straddled the fence[23] and still others adamantly denied that there could be any such thing.[24]

Fence-straddling results from a failure to follow the thought to its logical conclusion and is very vulnerable.[25] It can be classed with outright denial which results from a lack of appreciation of the incarnational principle and an overemphasis on the parish as an "administrative unit" of the Church.

In spite of the fact that "the Church should embody itself in concrete social forms adapted to human life,"[26] some writers refuse to apply fully the implications of the incarnational principle to the parish. They totally separate the supernatural from the natural and assert that only the divine makes theologizing possible. They overlook the obvious fact that the human condition is the locus of theology without which no revelation, no theology could ever have taken place.[27]

Those writers who reduce the parish to merely an administrative unit of the Church, on the other hand, justify their position by demonstrating that historically the parish developed as a response to specific human needs of the Church. Consequently, they argue, the parish is not regulated by revealed data but by canon law and should be dealt with as a sector of ecclesial administration and not as a bearer of theological truth.[28]

Obviously, both of the above groups of writers have failed to work out fully the implications of the incarnation. In theologizing about the parish, the *incarnational principle* should be a guiding light. This principle affirms that the human and divine are so intertwined that only when they are taken together is the theologian able to understand fully the nature and mission of the parish. After dealing with the parish as presented in the documents of Vatican II, we will analyze this important principle in greater depth.

2. The Parish in the Documents of Vatican II

Although local church in the documents primarily means the diocese and not the parish,[29] there are several texts that are significant for the theology of the parish. The Constitution on the Sacred Liturgy (SC) is the most explicit in this regard. Number 41 stresses the importance of the community in celebrating the liturgy together with its bishop, while number 42 situates the parish within the diocese as a theological reality, not as a mere administrative unit of Church-government.

The bishop is to be considered the high priest of his flock. In a certain sense it is from him that the faithful who are under his care derive and maintain their life in Christ.

Therefore all should hold in very high esteem the liturgical life of the diocese which centers around the bishop, especially in his cathedral church. Let them be persuaded that the Church reveals herself most clearly when the full complement of God's holy people, united in prayer and in common liturgical service (especially the Eucharist), exercise a thorough and active participation at the very altar where the bishop presides in the company of his priests and other assistants.

But because it is impossible for the bishop always and everywhere to preside over the whole flock in his Church, he cannot do other than establish lesser groupings of the faithful. Among these, parishes set up locally under a pastor who takes the place of the bishop are the most important: for in a certain way they represent the visible Church as it is established throughout the world.

Therefore the liturgical life of the parish and its relationship to the bishop must be fostered in the thinking and practice of both laity and clergy; efforts also must be made to encourage a sense of community within the parish, above all in the common celebration of the Sunday Mass.[30]

There is no legalistic element in this text. It is beautiful theology bringing back the patristic concept of the Eucharistic communion. Even the reference, "parishes set up locally under a pastor" is more theological than canonical for it implies both the undeniable spatial and temporal nature of any and all liturgical celebrations and their connection with the bishop. The bishop plays a central role in this text. All the different local groups indicated there, e.g., the diocesan assembly, the parochial community, and other possible liturgical gatherings, are envisioned in the text in their retionship with the bishop. He is "the high priest of his flock," presiding over the celebration either in person or through his priest-pastor-representative, He is, therefore, *a constitutive* element not only of the diocese but also of the parish and of other possible liturgical gatherings.

This constitutive role of the bishop is also stressed in the Dogmatic Constitution on the Church (LG) when it is affirmed that, owing to the fullness of the sacrament of orders present in the bishop, he either offers the Eucharist himself or causes it to be offered.[31] The inference from this theological understanding of the episcopal presence in the local celebrations is that any given form of the parish-structure is relevant, useful, and to be maintained only to the extent that it reflects and contributes to the actualization of the divine presence in concrete human situations. It can coincide with the diocese, as it did in the early centuries of Christianity, or it can be its subdivision. But whatever form it gains in the course of history, it is a parish only to the extent that it operates under the direct or indirect authority of the bishop for the sacramental concretization of the divine presence.

The Dogmatic Constitution on the Church (LG) is very explicit on this point. First, it underscores the bishop's role and authority in the diocese as such; then, it speaks of Christ's presence in the local celebrating communities. A careful reading of these texts leads us to conclude that, while the first paragraph may be interpreted exclusively in the diocesan context, the second paragraph clearly refers to parish communities in which every legitimate celebration of the Eucharist is regulated by the bishop.

> This Church of Christ is truly present in all legitimate local congregations of the faithful which, united with their pastors, are themselves called churches in the New Testament. For in their own locality these are the new people called by God, in the Holy Spirit and in much fullness (cf. 1 Thessalonians 1:5). In them the faithful are gathered together by the preaching of the gospel of Christ, and the mystery of the Lord's Supper is celebrated, "that by the flesh and blood of the Lord's body the whole brotherhood may be joined together."
>
> In any community existing around the altar, under the sacred ministry of the bishop, there is manifested a symbol of that charity and "unity of the Mystical Body, without which there can be no salvation." In these communities, though frequently small and poor, or living far from any other, Christ is present. By virtue of Him the one, holy, catholic, and apostolic Church gathers together. For "the partaking of the Body and Blood of Christ does nothing other than transform us into that which we consume."[32]

It might also be helpful to consider here some ideas of the Decree on the Bishops' Pastoral Office in the Church (CD), particularly number 30 which deals with pastors as shepherds "entrusted with the care of souls in a certain part of the diocese under the bishop's authority."[33] In this capacity, their teaching, sanctifying, and governing activities should be discharged in such a way as to make the parishioners feel that "they are members of the diocese and of the universal Church."[34] But not only the parishioners! The pastor, as the agent of both the diocese and the universal Church, can never be satisfied with reaching out only for the active parishioners. Not at all! In true missionary spirit he is to seek out "everyone living in the parish boundaries." And if he cannot do it himself, he must enlist the help of others, the laity among them.[35] Finally, this document makes it crystal clear that "the parish exists solely for the good of souls."[36] This good of souls even demands that a certain degree of stability be accorded to the pastors, although the Council has abrogated the concept of irremovability to enable the bishop to "better provide for the needs of the good of souls."[37]

3. Application of the Incarnational Principle

This theologico-pastoral approach to the parish is the natural outgrowth of the understanding of the Church as a divine-human reality in which both divine and human elements are to be considered important and constitutive because "they form one interlocked reality" that "is compared to the mystery of the incarnate Word."[38] The communal structure of the Church is thus very important for the nature and the understanding of the calling of the people of God, provided that it accomplishes what it has been called into existence for, i.e., to be the living instrument of Christ's Spirit in the building up of the Body in the same way as the human nature assumed by the Word became the living instrument of salvation. This communal structure can be neither denied nor neglected. But it is not to be overvalued either. A merely canonical approach is likely to do the latter while a theologico-pastoral outlook may keep it in its proper role and place.

It follows, furthermore, that the concrete form and the precise details of the human structure can never be defined once and for all. As man grows in consciousness and becomes increasingly more aware of his abilities and responsibilities;

as individual and social life evolves with the changing cultural background and rapid technological achievements, it is not only possible but also necessary that the precise structural form of the relationship of the human and the divine be questioned, reexamined, and reformulated. Language, the primary symbol for human communication, is a growing and developing reality itself. It is, indeed, fitting that its achievements, too, as the most natural vehicle of thought, be under continuous scrutiny and study—particularly when the human formulation of divine mysteries is at stake. And whenever we deal with the Church and its human structure, this unique problem weighs heavily in our theological formulations.

The parish stands out as a classical illustration of the difficulties flowing from the inadequacy of the human as a co-constitutive element of the Church. Yet it is essential to realize that whatever historical form the relationship of the divine and the human might take in the evolving Church, it is there to aid the Church in the realization of the presence of God's saving grace in human form, as the visible expression of the trinitarian love-relationships in human communion and brotherhood, and as the unfolding of the salvific divine plan in the history of the people of God.

> Since the Church is both immanent and transcendent, it must always be open, ready, and disposed to recommence its incarnation in new forms and in new historical and cultural contexts, and not link itself exclusively or indissolubly to any race or nation, to any one set of customs, to any particular way of life, old or new. Since the unity of the Church must be compatible with communion, brotherhood, and collegiality, it may not present itself in such a way that it seems to have no room for a real application of the principles of subsidiarity, immanence, and co-responsibility.[39]

But, above all, the Church is to remember that as the

pilgrim people of God marching on in history and contributing to the unfolding of the salvific plan of God, she is "a kind of sacrament or sign of intimate union with God, and of the unity of all mankind. She is also an instrument for the achieving of such union and unity."[40] The ecclesial function of achieving union with God and unity among men and women takes place, ordinarily, on the local level where the faithful first become aware of such a calling and then commit themselves to its realization in the sacramental operations of the Church.

> Since the Church is a communion in which all are brothers and truly equal in dignity, it may not be or represent itself as a monarchy, however well established, that never realizes how in fact all the baptized play a part in preserving the faith we have received. Since the universal Church really exists in the form of particular churches and on the basis of these, it may not organize itself primarily as a "universal" Church which demands subjection and uniformity of all members.[41]

We have seen above that some object to a theology of the parish on the ground that the latter is an ecclesiastical institution, subject to radical change.[42] Nobody can deny this fact. Nevertheless, the historical nature of the parish negates its theological reality only if one intends to take this local, concretized community as an object of theological reflection in itself rather than in dependence on the diocese and the universal Church. Such an effort is an anomaly even if one builds one's case on a solely canonical approach to the problem. We feel that this is the downfall of such a concept of the parish. In their legalistic approach to it as a territorially limited administrative unit of the Church, these writers fail to see that whatever historical form it may be vested in at different times and in different places, the parish remains the principal gathering place of the faithful for the sacramental celebration of Christ's presence among them. The canonical form is not of its essence.

It is, however, essential to its very being that the parish always operate under the bishop and within the diocese as an eventful celebration of the whole Body of Christ. Neither does it have to seek the creation of a sociologically, hence "locally limited community,"[43] as some claim. But it certainly seeks, and hopefully succeeds in forming, a spiritually unified communion of all those who listen to the Word of God and celebrate the Eucharist together, and who care about one another. Yet the stress lies always more on what is to be accomplished in the Spirit of Christ rather than on what kind of sociological homogeneity is desirable or possible within the territorial limits of the parish.

> We have to see the Church as missionary in an organic sense. This has a greater affinity to the more precise meaning of the word *universal* as a gathering-together-in-oneness (uni-versal). The Church does not so much spread outward as draw inward. She is more a "presence" in the world than a widespread organization. The more she is present in the life of the world as its underlying principle of unity, the more evident is the fact that her action is supremely that of animation. She does not usurp, dominate, impose, or destroy; she fulfils. She supplies contemporary social life with the only sufficiently spiritual inspiration or impetus, and this will bring it to its final term as the way of life in which the people who enjoy it will find their highest aspirations as human beings.[44]

We are now in a better position for dealing with some of the main theological approaches to the nature of the parish. The spirit and the pastoral direction of Vatican II make their study a bit easier and our conclusion more plausible.

4. Efforts toward a Theology of the Parish

Approach of Early Liturgists

To establish the starting point for the modern reflections on the theology of the parish the 1920s and 1930s seem to be the most promising years[45] because some liturgical writers of that time developed the image of the parish as the Church in miniature. A. Wintersig, trying to overcome the exclusively legalistic and sociological approach to the parish, went on to build his reflections on the reality of the Incarnation and the Mystical Body of Christ and then drew the inference that the parish should be understood as the integral cell of the whole which unites and mirrors the entire Body.[46] He even attributed a certain temporal priority to the parish vis-à-vis the diocese by claiming the baptismal font as the maternal womb in which the Christian is conceived and developed while the diocese is embraced by the baptized only in the sacrament of Confirmation. The culminating point of Christian life is reached in the Eucharistic celebration, for the altar symbolizes Christ and the two become the cornerstone of Christian life in the parish.[47]

Wintersig's concept of the parish as the Church in miniature led to further claims and theological conceptualizations. On the one hand, the parish was simply identified with the Church;[48] on the other, it was represented by a new terminology as *Ecclesiola in Ecclesia*. M. Schurr describes this concept very vividly in presenting the Church as a concentrically constructed reality.

As a collapsible cup is made of separate rings which fit closely into one another and only form a drinking vessel when they are properly assembled: so it is also with the structure of holy Church which consists of four concentric communities constituting the visible organization of our Lord's Body. First there is the outermost ring, the unity of the all-embracing universal Church. The second ring is the episcopate:

though founded by divine law its concrete form is defined by canon law. The third ring is the parish, also created by the law of the Church. The fourth ring, finally, is the divine institution of the family sanctified by the sacrament of matrimony and itself consisting of individual Christian personalities.[49]

Both these views, however, were made possible by the liturgical convictions, aspirations, claims, and trends of those years. Real enthusiasm for liturgical understanding of and participation in the sacramental life of the Church favored such theological developments. The liturgical movement even further stimulated theological investigation by over-emphasizing the nature and the role of the parish.

The first reaction to the Church-in-miniature-proposition naturally came from the canonists. O. V. Nell-Breuning built his case on the Code. He argued that the parish cannot even be considered as a community since canon law offers no such concept.[50] The only permissible way of dealing with the parish is dictated by its very nature: it is the primary means for "orderly pastoral care." One cannot go beyond that. It is an administrative unit of the diocese and not a proper object of theology.

This re-emergence of the legalistic understanding and interpretation of the parish on one side and the liturgical overemphasis of the celebrating parish-community on the other did not settle the original problem. The either/or methodology, with its frustrations and exaggerations, promised nothing but despair and sterility. More experiences were needed to bend the unyielding positions, and deeper theological insights were sought to make the inquiries more promising and more fruitful.

French and German Experiences

The new experiences came from France via developments just before, during, and mostly right after World War II. While in Germany theological thought concerning the parish was greatly influenced by the suppression of Catholic organizations by Hitler, French thought was generated by the Church's loss of the working class. Accordingly, while the German approach to the problem developed more on the theoretical than the practical level, the French vision of the parish was entirely pastoral, practical, and concrete in nature without lacking, however, theological depth or historical perspective. The names of H. Godin,[51] G. Michonneau,[52] Cardinal M. Feltin[53] represent the French orientation and interest in the parish. The parish as mission dominated their outlook, determined their immediate aim, and guided their hope. Because of this predominantly pastoral attitude and priestly apostolate as well as the lack of systematic methodology and the power of analysis, they could not and did not attempt a theological synthesis of the parish. Nevertheless, it is to their credit that, without using Karl Rahner's term, their outlook clearly recognized the anonymous-Christian-situation in war-torn France. Michonneau's vision justifies our claim.

> If you consider as 'real Christians' everyone who has been baptized, or even only those who made their First Communion and had, in childhood, some degree of contact with the Church, then the problem is solved. The 'mass' in France is Christian; there is no 'mission territory' in France. But if we wish to restrict the title of Christian (and we are not saying 'good Christians') to those who have the Faith, to those to whom Christ is a reality, we must have the courage to stand by the opinion of 'France, a Mission Land', and that the mass of the working class *is* pagan. Not because they do not practice the Faith, but because (and the evidence is so clear on this point that we are amazed at any discussion of it) their mentality is pagan and completely foreign to the Christian spirit, indifferent to our creed and careless of the demands of our moral code.[54]

The German and French experiences were not the only ones giving prominence to the role and function of the parish in pre- and post-World War II years. But they were certainly the most influential ones, protruding heavily in the disturbed consciences of the theologians of those two countries. Naturally, therefore, some of the most significant thoughts on the theology of the parish have been developed and promoted by them.

Yves Congar

Yves Congar was the first systematic theologian to try to translate the French and German experiences into a theology of the parish.[55] His ideas on the subject became so well-known and so widely-discussed that they have influenced practically every theologian interested in the nature of the parish since 1948. For Congar, the parish is more than an administrative unit of the universal and the diocesan Church. It is even more than a celebrating community realized around the altar in the liturgico-sacramental operations. Though he likes and appreciates the characterization of the parish by A. Wintersig as a liturgical person—*une personne liturgique*—he claims that the theologian must go beyond the merely liturgical approach to the parish to discover its theological content.

To do this, he first sets the problem in focus by describing the parish as an organism that, unlike the diocese, is neither essential nor indispensable to the nature of the Church.[56] Actually, the diocese could exist without the parish structure and did so up to the sixth century. Diocese and parish were simply identical. On no level of the ecclesial structure is the parish needed *per se*. History shows that the East tried to go without it by creating the *chorepiscopi* instead. One is, therefore, justified in claiming that it was human need and not the nature of the Church as such that called for the creation of the parish-system.

What, then, is the parish for Congar? How does he define it? It is the spiritual counterpart of the natural grouping of a certain number of independent families in the solidarity of everyday existence.[57] Correspondingly, the parish can be compared, from the viewpoint of function, to the family while the diocese would have its counterpart in the city.[58] Though it can be said that the Church is both family and city on every level of her being and structure, Congar finds the distinction between the two organisms, parish and diocese, valid and theologically relevant. As the family is the natural milieu of and the most important contributing factor to a child's becoming an adult, so the parish is the generative and formative milieu of a human person's becoming a Christian.

This formation is basic and elementary, without being preoccupied with preparation for specific aspects of the Christian life. In Congar's words, it is a fundamental formation, *sine addito,* concentrated on the essential elements of one's Christian life, incorporation into the Body of the Lord. The baptismal font in the parish church symbolizes this radically basic function that is translated into practicality in the ordinary sacramental operations, in catechetical and homiletical instructions, and, eminently, in the formation of the conscience of each individual Christian. Following Congar's line of thought, one could say that the parish is really and truly the hearth, the sanctuary, of the formation of Christian personalities, "the maternal womb out of which the Christian as such is born, the Christian *sine addito,* the Christian without further distinguishing characteristics, just as the human being as such is born in the bosom of the family."[59]

The city, on the other hand, puts into motion a higher and more specific development of human life by providing opportunities for his growth and differentiation, by offering job-opportunities, and by regulating community life by laws and coercion.[60] Accordingly, the bishop and the diocesan structure transcend the maternal role of the parish, create higher roles and structures for the people, introduce differentiation and distribution of offices, and provide for all the needs that transcend the homogeneous atmosphere of the parish.

The parish, then, in Congar's understanding, plays an educational role in the life of the Christian by developing his interior life, by training him in the spirit of charity, and by helping him realize his concrete responsibilities. In this basic educational process Congar follows faithfully his understanding of the Church as an incarnational reality. Truth (doctrine, dogma), grace (sacraments), and power (authority), given to the believers, and symbolized by the Congarian term *Ecclesia de Trinitate,* make up the divine element in the Church; the society of the believers, characterized by the term *Ecclesia ex hominibus,* is the human element; these two together, in concrete human existence, form the *Ecclesia in Christo,* the believing community here and now.[61]

In a 1948 pioneering address[62] on the parish Congar built on the same idea with a slightly different terminology by affirming that the community of believers, particularly in its concrete parochial form, is constructed from above (*d'en haut*) and from below (*d'en bas*). The former represents whatever divine element enters into the forming of the ecclesial community—truth, grace, power. These are called the objective elements of salvation. Though they are most important in the spiritual makeup of man, in themselves they are not enough. These divine elements need to be handed over to people to fashion them into a living community. For the Church, while being an institution of divine realities, is also a community of the redeemed. Here is found the element from below, the community of men. But community for Congar entails more than just the living side by side. It also signifies more than docile submission to the directives and initiatives of the head-person. Community means people interested and actively involved in collectivity. It is interaction of all with all. Its law is to act with others.[63]

The parish is, therefore, a basis for elementary, ground-breaking operation, an initial and vital unity of community life, reflecting, in the supernatural sphere, the natural human reality in its process of growth, and this is exactly what makes it so valuable in the eyes of Congar for the life of the Church. No, he does not claim that the Church is made up of parish-base-units as their sum total, so to speak. He nevertheless notes without hesitation, that in a certain sense she could be looked upon as made up of parishes somehow in the same way as a nation is made up of families.[64]

As might be expected, Congar's theory of the parish encountered doubting Thomases and outright objections. One valid objection is that "the analogy with the family-State relation does not provide a properly theological statement on the parish."[65] Also true, when properly nuanced, is the remark that "the Christian *sine addito*, the Christian without further distinguishing marks, is an abstraction."[66] Yet the parish-family comparison, while not theological in the traditional sense, is not entirely without foundation and significance. The generative and formative elements, the important primary relationships in fashioning a human personality, are also vital factors in one's becoming a Christian. Such a pace-setting process cannot take place in a vacuum. And Congar deserves credit for trying to change the then-prevailing canonical or exclusively liturgical view of the parish as early as 1948 and replacing it with a theologically meaningful image that could be useful in the re-Christianization process of the French Church and also generate further thought and research in theological circles.

In any case, the basic problem lies not so much in Congar's family-parish parallel as in the fact that his critics completely missed the meaning of his Church "from above." In their eyes, the Church from above is a hierarchical structure extending right down to the parish. The Church is formed through the hierarchical mediation.[67] By leaving out Congar's understanding of grace and truth, such criticism not only truncates Congar's genuine concept of the *Ecclesia de Trinitate*, but—what is worse—also stresses the hierarchical aspect out of proportion. For if the Church is formed through hierarchical mediation it is important to know what mediation is about.

Finally, we appreciate least the claim that the parish cannot without more ado be said to be a community.[68] As we have already mentioned above, the community is not something already statically established; it is always in the continuous process of becoming. This is particularly true of a spiritual communion which is not necessarily best interpreted by sociological charts and graphics.

To sum up, it is important to realize that Congar's concept of the parish was a pioneering effort in the 1940s. As such, it generated further thoughts and made possible counter-efforts in describing the same reality. To judge it, therefore, in the light of later developments, instead of analyzing it as a brave and creative venture in itself, is a step in the wrong direction. Without it, the theology of the parish would have suffered immeasurably.

Karl Rahner

To understand Rahner's interest in and approach to the theology of the parish, it is advisable to recall, first, his concept of the diaspora Church. As early as 1961 he already saw clearly that "the form of the Church's existence in public life is changing"[69] owing to a new feature of contemporary society, for "a Christian has to live his Christianity among a large number of non-Christians."[70] The consequences of this historical development are eye-opening and, to many people, even disappointing.

1) The Christian's "faith is constantly threatened from without." Society is not supportive of religious beliefs and practices. Each individual has to achieve them on his own as the outcome of his personal decision. "By and large the situation will remain one of choice, not of natural growth, of a personal achievement constantly renewed amid perilous surroundings."[71]

2) The literary, artistic, and scientific elements of culture which form the immediate and necessary milieu of Christian life and "upon which a Christian too lives and *must* live" not only are specifically non-Christian but also exercise "a negative influence on a Christian's moral life."[72]

3) To stay alive in this situation the Church must depend on "a laity conscious of itself as bearing the Church in itself, as constituting her, and not being simply an object for her— i.e., the clergy—to look after her."[73]

4) As a consequence, the clergy will no longer belong to the upper level of society; the priesthood will cease to be a status-symbol.[74]

5) Rahner also notes that the diaspora-situation will lessen if not eliminate all conflicts between the Church and the state. Instead of solving such conflicts on the levels of the two societies, they have to be solved by individual Christians in the sanctuary of their consciences.[75]

These situational premises, then, enable Rahner to draw conclusions from them,[76] the most important of which must be the realization by the believers that "we cannot cease to be missionary." But missionary in what sense? Coming close to the reality of the parish, Rahner sounds very practical, as he writes,

If we live in the diaspora, then the office-job type of pastor will have to die out. For the only service available from the bureaucrat mentality, which does still exist, is one that has no real care for the public: a service of an institution, not of people. Have we the courage to break away from bureaucracy, office hours, routine, impersonal, non-functional organizational clutter and clerical machinery—and just do pastoral work? If a man can find in us another man, a real Christian, with a heart, someone who cares about him and is really delivering the message of God's mercy towards us sinners, then more is happen-

ing than if we can hear the impressive and unmistak-
able hum of bureaucratic machinery. Let us get away
from the tyranny of statistics. For the next hundred
years they are always going to be against us, if we
ever let them speak out of turn. *One* real conversion
in a great city is something more splendid than the
spectacle of a whole remote village going to the
sacraments. The one is an essentially religious event,
a thing of grace; the other is to a large extent a
sociological phenomenon, even though it may be a
means of God's grace."

What kind of theological understanding of the parish
is possible in this diaspora-situation? Even before Rahner
worked out his diaspora-concept, he had already been reflecting on the nature of the parish, and has continued read-
justing and reformulating it ever since.[78] A subtle develop-
ment-process can, therefore, be easily detected in his train
of thought. While in 1948 he was quite in line with the
canonical posture in working out the parochial-principle
without ever subscribing to its absolute application or excessive claims, later writings have brought out his most
profound and beautiful insights into the theology of the
parish even before Vatican II.

First of all, he takes the clear position that a theologian
cannot be satisfied with either an exclusively canonical
definition or a mere general ecclesiology if he intends to
speak meaningfully about the parish. Where can he, then,
turn for an answer? How should he proceed? This is how
Rahner answers the question.

From the very beginning, one could suspect that only
if the Church as a whole enters into consideration
can the parish as such be a genuine object of theology.
For only the Church can be a primary and original
object of theology; that is, an object instituted by
Christ and divinely revealed. But, on the other hand,

if we are to do more than merely repeat the general statements of ecclesiology, the idea of the parish itself must come into play. These two prerequisites can only be united if we can find a theological bond or relation between the Church, as a proper object of theology, and the parish; and this relation must say more than the mere canonical establishment of parishes by ecclesiastical authority.[79]

Rahner defines this relationship by saying that "the parish is in a very definite sense the representative actuality of the Church. The Church appears and manifests itself in the event of the central life of the parish."[80]

This definition implies two fundamental theses. The first is that "the Church, as event, is necessarily a local and localized community."[81] He affirms the continuing existence of the Church and advocates that it becomes more fully actualized in its juridically founded and structured society. The Church, by being such a society, in addition to its continued existence, also acts and by acting she achieves a higher degree of actuality than by merely preserving her existence. Now, this actually takes place on the local level in teaching, praying, offering the Sacrifice, etc. Therefore, the permanence and historical continuity of the enduring Church supposes and requires "placeness" for all sacramental operations, particularly for the Eucharistic celebration because "the Eucharist can be celebrated only by a community which is gathered together in one and the same place... All this means that the Church, in its innermost essence, is itself directed to a localized concretization; and this in no way harms or lessens its universal destiny and mission to all men."[82]

The second thesis goes a step further and claims that the parish is the *primary* realization of the Church as event.[83] This second thesis is necessary for Rahner to distinguish the parish from other "local community" celebrations, such as those of a monastic community, youth group, etc. These, too, are celebrations "of a local community in which the total Church becomes event. However, the parish is still *de facto* and *de jure* the primary, normal, and original form of local community—and this simply because the parish exists by the principle of place alone."[84] Here again we find Rahner's concept of placeness as constitutive of the parish. Although he notes with objectivity that other possible local structures might and actually did emerge in the course of history, he still maintains that "this placeness of the human situation causes the greatest historical realization of man's supernatural salvation and life to be itself local."[85]

Is *placeness* really so important in our understanding of the parish? Rahner, in his effort to clarify the issue, first distinguishes "the placeness of the celebrating community as such" from "the generally presupposed common placeness of those coming together for this Eucharistic celebration,"[86] and then states that, though separable in themselves, they actually "belong together because people do not usually come together for the Mass, as such, if they ordinarily live in different places."[87] This togetherness of placenesses is most prominent in the parish structure because it alone lives exclusively from the principle of localness (placeness) and is, therefore, the primary local community. It really grows out of the very nature of man who can exist only as having a home.[88]

While recognizing the subtle and profound nature of Rahner's train of thoughts, his critics suggest that what he has given us here is a theology of the local community rather than a theology of the parish as such.[89] This objection, however, is without foundation after Vatican II since the Council, by characterizing the parish as the most important among the lesser groupings of the faithful, has practically invited theologians to subject it to theological investigations.

There is, however, another objection which seems to be more serious and to the point. Rahner's critics maintain that man's nature does not warrant basing the primary form of the supernatural local community of the Eucharistic celebration on the mere fact of living together in one place.[90] They even carry this argument further by insisting that the liturgy of itself does not create or form a locally limited community.[91] Now, this is an argument against something Rahner has not even tried to establish. His argument goes from the placeness or at-homeness of man to the placeness of the liturgy, not *vice versa*. At least, not in the sense of claiming sociological at-homeness. A spiritual community does not necessarily coincide and should not be confused with a "locally limited community."

Yet the problems rooted in the concept of placeness continued to preoccupy Rahner, and eventually he returned to them in a later work to clarify the territorial principle. He affirms that it "can never be the sole foundation of the parish, just as it can never be the only foundation of a diocese" since a personal parish—for example, a national parish—can have as much justification for its existence as a territorial parish. He even adds pointedly:

> It can be an equally concrete embodiment of the function of the bishop and diocese; this kind of non-territorial community of worshipers united by personal and professional bonds can be of far greater Christian significance than the more artificial society created by the neighborhood in which the parishioners happen to live.[92]

What, then, is the *raison d'etre* of the parish? Apparently Rahner, after much reflection and analysis and after having taken into consideration the bishop's role in the life of the people of God, was able to better balance his theological understanding of the parish by stressing more the liturgical than the territorial aspect of the local gatherings. For if it is true that the powers of sanctification belong to every bishop in the Church, it is also true that those powers must be exercised everywhere in the Church. Therefore:

The Church must appear in every local Church, and

the greatest celebration of the presence of redemption and of the Church itself, the Eucharist, must be found everywhere. Consequently, the powers which make possible such total presence of the Church in every locality cannot themselves be tied down geographically.[92]

This means that the bishop, in delegating some of his powers for the good of the Church, can do so in either of two ways: by limiting the delegation to a particular group of persons (personal principle), or by limiting it to clearly defined territories (territorial principle). It is even possible that the future will offer some new forms of participation in the bishop's powers. The ever-changing situation of society could create such demands in the ever-changing situation of the Church. Yet one thing must always remain constant in the midst of change.

What is immutable in all of the Church's new historical forms is that these offices are participations in the mission of the bishop and remain subordinate to him. . . . This framework of divine law is ultimately built into the nature of the Church itself so that official powers can be transmitted in a great variety of combinations and degrees, as the age we live in demands.[94]

At the end of the reflections, Rahner's concept of the parish, though still territorially oriented, is clearly aligned with the centrality of the altar for proclaiming the Word of God and celebrating the Eucharist. It is his response to a heterogeneous situation created by the diaspora-Church, and a consequence of the fact that the Eucharist is always linked to a place. Because of this placeness, the bishop's altar is not the only one in the diocese. And also because of this placeness "the local liturgical congregation is the essence of the parish."

Since the Eucharist cannot be celebrated unless a number of people come together in the same place, the most normal situation is for those Christians who live together in the same neighborhood to come together at the same altar. The social and individual significance of living together in a local community has no doubt been very different at different times. In today's urban society locale is much less important because home, place of work, centers of social life, of leisure activities, of culture, etc., are becoming increasingly independent of one another. The proximity of homes which may be little more than places to eat and sleep is not at all the same thing as the home environment of villages and small towns which used to form the natural liturgical community. Yet even today physical neighborhood still has human, personal significance, and for our celebration of the Eucharist on weekday mornings or evenings and on Sundays and holy days it is normally the almost indispensable natural condition of a community of worshipers.[95]

Casiano Floristan

In 1964 an interesting book appeared on the American market: *The Parish—Eucharistic Community*, a translation from the Spanish original.[96] Though it did not create great waves in the ocean of theological thought, it is a significant and stimulating theological achievement.

Floristan, after dealing with the concept of the parish in the Bible and in history, undertakes the theological study of both the Church as the Mystical Body of Christ and the diocese as "the local concentration of the universal Church."[97] On these grounds, he then sets out to construe a theology of the parish itself as the local Eucharistic community. By reviewing, evaluating, and criticizing the main efforts preceding his in dealing with the parish—Congar and Rahner among them—he builds up his arguments suggesting the Eucharistic community as a fitting concept of the parish. We are interested in this aspect of his work.

Floristan's basic doctrinal supposition is the claim, hardly defensible after Vatican II, that not only is the Church built on the incarnational principle, but it is the continuation of the Incarnation of Christ on earth.[98] This continued Incarnation takes place in the parish in virtue of the two supernatural elements, the Word of God and the Eucharist, mediated to the community of the faithful through their principal agent, the bishop. This is a beautiful conclusion drawn by Floristan from studies preceding his own. However, his contribution to the inquiry is hardly to be found in his conclusion. His original pattern of thought is rather prominent in some of his doctrinal suppositions leading to a complete vision of the parish.

Particularly insightful is his treatment of the relationship of revelation and situation—human condition would have been a much better term—which virtually contains the germ of a concept to be discussed shortly. He speaks of two loyalties, one to principles, to revelation, and to God; the other, to the situation, to real persons, and to the communities of life. The theandric nature of the Church simply demands these two loyalties since the model of all ecclesial action is the twin nature of Jesus Christ. So far so good. Unfortunately, he does not stop here. He goes further and states that Jesus Christ "lived in space, was subject to time, and in His human nature had a psychic and social constitution similar to that of man. The Church, the permanent incarnation of the Son of God, reproduces Jesus Christ."[99]

However, it is difficult to understand and interpret, first, his concept of the Church as the "permanent incarnation" that reproduces Jesus Christ, and secondly, his human elements in the divine-human duality. As soon as he steps beyond the incarnational principle, and claims continuation of the Incarnation, he passes from the togetherness of the divine and the human in the saving plan of God to a techni-

cal relationship of Jesus' divinity to His humanity paralleled
in the nature of the Church.

Let us suppose that the parallel is really there: in what
specific element is the human, the counterpart of the divine,
recognized? In the visible hierarchy? Or in the spatial, temporal, and social constitution of the Church? Or, perhaps,
in the secular aspect that ties it to the world? In a few lines
Floristan refers to all these factors, and we fear that the
shaky foundation on which he has built his conclusion for
the theology of the parish might itself destroy his conclusion.[100] For what he himself says concerning man in space,
in society, in time, and man as a psychic phenomenon,[101] and
what he wants to say theologically about the parish is better
conveyed by the incarnational principle than by his concept
of a *continued Incarnation*.

Our study of Floristan can be concluded by quoting his
own most explicit definition of the parish. Owing to his subtle
distinction, however, between "substantially present" and
"substantially and fully present," one may wonder whether
it was in fact the parish or the diocese that guided him in
formulating his definition.

> The parish is the local community which celebrates
> the Eucharist. . . . The pastor is a priest who celebrates
> the Eucharist with a power inherent in his priesthood
> but with a permission that continuously depends on
> the bishop. The Church is substantially present in the
> parochial eucharistic celebration but not in all its
> manifestations. It is substantially and fully present
> as a local church at the pontifical Mass when the bish-
> op is surrounded by his *presbyterium*. The pontifical
> liturgy is so rich and solemn because of the fact that
> the local church resides in the bishop, especially when
> he celebrates the Eucharist.[102]

Alex Blöchlinger

In the debate concerning the nature of a parish and

specifically the possibility of a theology of the parish, Blöchlinger[103] can be characterized as the leading proponent of the negative school among theologians,[104] just as von Nell-Breuning is among canonists.[105] In his eyes, the theological approach is no more successful in creating a parish community than the canonical approach. In an evaluating overview, so to speak, Blöchlinger sums up the theological statements about the parish in this way:

> The most important ones affirm that the supernatural reality of the Church must incarnate itself in human structures; that the universal Church is essentially manifested in the local eucharist; that the parish as territory is a part of the bishop's powers; that the parish in the strictly canonical sense is a human institution, but that beyond and before it, the supernatural reality of the Church and the diocese is alive in it. The supernatural reality is indeed present and active in the parish but it is not the parish and must be clearly distinguished from it.[106]

Wherein, then, does the problem lie? In the specific question raised by Blöchlinger and in the answer given to it by him: Do these statements allow the theologian to speak of "parish community"? No, he answers, because

> the supernatural reality which we find in the parish *ipso facto* includes as such also supernatural community. Christian faith and Christian life are unthinkable without community. But this supernatural community cannot of itself be characterized as parish community.[107]

One feels that Blöchlinger and his followers are fighting the wrong issue when, after their initial acceptance of the Church as a supernatural-natural, invisible-visible, identical-pluralistic, divine-human, hence incarnational community, they question whether supernatural community can gain expression as parish community. For they do so simply because of the presence of differences in community-links, originated and rooted in human structure. Admittedly, it is easy to claim but very hard to realize any community in our human condition. But the difficult is not impossible. It is potentially there, always ready to take place to some extent and in some degree—particularly when the Spirit of the Lord is working at it.

Blöchlinger's phrase of "a closed and distinctive community,"[108] is unfortunate because it could create the impression that the parish community is separate from both the diocesan and universal community. Such a concept would negate the very essence of the parish. But if he means a concrete, local community in which both the diocese and the universal Church *actualize here and now* in the intensive concentration of the Spirit of the Lord, we have no objection to his understanding of the parish on this point.

In general, his methodology and his adamant negating of a theology of the parish even after a long and painstaking study of the nature and meaning of the liturgy are puzzling. Admittedly, he does not reject the concept of the parish as an outmoded remnant of ancient times. On the contrary, he reaffirms it vigorously. But he does so more on canonical than on theological grounds.

> The canonical parish is open to the supernatural reality of the Church and can be shaped by the changing forms of the world; it is still valid and still has its value as a legal institution. The legal form is in itself adaptable enough to embrace a parish 'congregation' and a parish community and yet to remain responsible for all those who are not yet touched by them. The legal term is by and large flexible enough to be adapted to modern sociological conditions.[109]

This might have sounded fine and beautiful in 1962, but it is out of place in these post-Vatican II times.

5. A New Approach to the Problem

The above approaches to and theories of the parish in a certain sense are puzzling, confusing, even bewildering. Clearly, in spite of the many beautiful thoughts, theological reflections, and pastoral conclusions present in these efforts, the debate itself has been conducted in the abstract, leaving behind the very existential situations which had been responsible for generating the debate in the first place. The threat of a Manichean or Gnostic dualism concerning the divine and human elements of the ecclesial reality of the parish has hovered, so to speak, over the discussions. For if the objection can be upheld that a theology of the parish is impossible because the latter is only a historical development and not a divinely established structure in the Church, the methodology of inquiry is dominated more by Manichean or Gnostic convictions than by the correct application of the incarnational principle.

In order to counteract this objection we will present the human condition as a locus of theology, then reformulate the principle of the Incarnation by working into it the eschatological point of view. In so doing, we will establish the theological basis and framework for possible contemporary models for the parish.

The Human Condition as Locus of Theology[110]

H. Godin, G. Michonneau, Cardinal M. Feltin, and others felt the pressure of the human condition in France, especially in Paris, and tried to look for a *new* theological orientation to and an effective working plan for the parish. The result was their understanding of the parish as a missionary community. A. Blöchlinger, unconvinced by theological and liturgical efforts toward solving the same problem, turned to sociology claiming that "in as far as the worshiping community is to permeate and form the natural community and be carried on by this community, other criteria must be found which can determine the effect of the worshiping community in the non-worshiping sphere. These criteria are to be found in sociology."[111] Floristan, too, sensed the problem of the human condition when he declared that, though theology, having the Bible and tradition as its points of departure, is not deduced from human events,

> ... each time a new phenomenon occurs theology should be there on the spot to consider it from the point of view of its own special criteria of observation. In this sense theology either is current or else is not universal theology. It cannot be absent from the *vox temporis*, just as the voice of history will not be true unless listened to in the light of the *lumen aeternitatis*. Failure to make theology current is as dangerous as not meditating on current events theologically. What is more, for us there is such a bond between situation and revelation, between time and eternity, between divine and human nature, between *caro* and *Verbum*, that theology cannot follow a situation but must instead precede it.[112]

The last sentence of the quotation seems to negate the grave implications of the entire statement and is, to some degree, up for interpretation. The quotation itself, however, indicates a great degree of sensitivity on Floristan's part even though the term situation can hardly be equated with the human condition as such.

The only one who has really pinpointed the problem, and has done his very best to formulate a theology of the parish in view of it, is Rahner. His diaspora-Church concept, his placeness and at-homeness, always so important in the operation of the parish, demonstrate a tremendous awareness of a new reality in the mind of contemporary man that has to be dealt with carefully but effectively even though no one at the present time can foresee all its possible implications for Christianity and the Church.

How is the human condition related to theology? It may bring about a fresh perspective on whatever is meant by human as the vehicle of the divine.

> While it was customary for the Christian theologian in the past to start theologizing with the data of revelation, today it is understood that all Christian theology must have a double datum for its starting point: supernatural revelation and the human condition.[113]

Again, a glance at the documents of Vatican II will enable the reader to find the framework for such a claim.

The Pastoral Constitution on the Church in the Modern World sets the stage for recognizing the importance of the human condition by taking a very affirmative stance toward real human values in general. It is the duty of the people of God, motivated by faith,

> to decipher authentic signs of God's presence and purpose in the happenings, needs, and desires in which this People has a part along with other men of our age. For faith throws a new light on everything, manifests God's design for man's total vocation, and thus directs the mind to solutions which are fully human.[114]

How can this be done? First, by assessing the highly prized values of today and by relating them to their divine source knowing that, "insofar as they stem from endowments conferred by God on man, these values are exceedingly good."[115]

Second, the position of man as the "center and crown" of all things on earth has to be established, in his relatedness, however, not in isolation, for "by his innermost nature man is a social being, and unless he relates himself to others he can neither live nor develop his potential."[116]

Third, since Christ died for all men, "by His incarnation the Son of God has united Himself in some fashion with every man."[117]

It is to be noted, too, that in the Declaration on the Relationship of the Church to Non-Christian Religions the Council gave primary consideration "to what human beings have in common and to what promotes fellowship among them," knowing that the profound mysteries of the human condition, "today even as in olden times, deeply stir the human heart."[118] This stirring takes place not only in virtue of creation, but also as a result of redemption in Christ. For the Church's "missionary activity is closely bound up ... with human nature itself and its aspirations. By manifesting Christ, the Church reveals to men the real truth about their condition and their total vocation. For Christ is the source and model of that renewed humanity ... to which all aspire."[119]

The reader might claim, and rightly so, that these pronouncements by Vatican II remain very general in nature and say nothing specific about the human condition as a locus of theology. Yet the positive attitude of the documents toward purely human values has had a twofold influence on theological development. On the one hand, the Council did not say no to research and affirmations already claiming human condition as a locus.[120] On the other, it tacitly gave approval to further study in this direction. The examination of the history of the Church, the analysis of doctrinal development and, most importantly, the comparative study of religions in this century have brought home the understanding that the human condition cannot be pushed into the background in the Christian economy of salvation.

> The invitation extended to man to participate in divine life as the result of the creation effected by Christ does not take place in a sort of abstract or ideal world, but in the world man experiences in and around himself every day of his earthly mission. The fact that Christ Himself adapted the human condition as the framework of His Incarnation and Redemption is eminent testimony not to the suppression or the disregard of the former, but to its ennobled,

exalted new significance in the economy of sacramental operation.[121]

Such an outlook is particularly important and significant
for the main topic of this study, the theology of the parish.
To refer again to Rahner's anonymous-Christian concept,
it can be stated plainly on the ground of experience that
on the parish-level the presence of non-Christian, and at
times possibly anti-Christian or even atheistic, convictions
and attitudes is evident. Christians of faith and conviction
live and work together with sociological Christians, non-
Christians, religiously uninterested individuals. Hence, if
there is anything the parish can offer to these people, it is
the God who reveals Himself in the human condition rather
than the God of positive revelation. The weight of this simple
fact pressures the theologian to consider the parish as a
worthy object of theological reflection precisely because
it is also a genuine milieu of the human condition.[122]
It must be evident by now that to speak of the human
condition is not to project it as something destructive or
even simply antagonistic to the supernatural-transcendent
reality of God. On the contrary, it is a revelatory agent of
the transcendent. Outside the Judeo-Christian world, it is
most likely to be the only such agent. This fact can hardly
be questioned by anyone, and objections to it usually are
not raised on this level. Resistance to the proposition develops with the further claim that the human condition continues to be important and to play a role even in the Judeo-
Christian reality of the people of God, as a partial agent of
the revelatory process. In this dimension, the human condition is not to be isolated as *the* primary factor or source.
Its role and influence are to be studied in the Spirit of the
Lord. Nevertheless, the diaspora-situation can give it prominence in many people's lives as the primary agent for guiding
them toward their light of origin and salvation.[123]
The possible consequences of such a position are incalculable for the parish. Christ and the human condition meet;

they are primarily experienced on this level. The dialogue between the two in the consciences of the believing or the sociological Christians starts here, and its outcome reverberates in the convictions, attitudes, and existential choices of the parishioners. The initial address to the human person could come from either source, but it is the quality of the given response that will determine whether the responder intends to structure his life as guided by the human condition alone or by the combined effort of the human and the divine.

This unceasing process of addressing and responding, of questioning and answering, of proclaiming and listening, of becoming aware of something and judgment-making, of initiating and educating those on whom the future of the people of God and of mankind will depend is the most commonly known feature in the contemporary parish. It displays both the pain of the human condition and the call of the Spirit of Christ, and invites those who do care about both to work out models that do not separate, but unify these vital realities in the lives of the parishioners. Proclaiming the Word of God, handing over Christian tradition, educating the young, and forming a Christian community in an un-Christian atmosphere can be successful only if being Christian also responds to what is most genuinely human in man.

Can we really say that the purpose of Christian education is to teach the youngsters of today how to become good Church-members of tomorrow? Or should we not rather advocate that, though Church-membership is an important element of human life, it is secondary to the preeminence of the human person and becomes meaningful only in view and in the service of the latter? For any institutionalized element found in the web of human existence was introduced there with the unique purpose to achieve something, i.e., to promote the good and the well-being of the individual human persons who actually make up the web. This primacy and preeminence must be clearly understood and unhesitatingly embraced by all concerned to-day.[124]

The Incarnational-Eschatological Principle

On taking the human condition seriously into consideration as a locus of theology, we see that the mere raising of the question leads us to inquire into what is really *normative* in the life of the Church. To put it another way, discussion of the human condition gives rise to the very important question as to whether giving a positive response to deep-seated human needs, hopes, and aspirations will ever endanger that which makes Christianity what it is.

The same question was asked somehow at a colloquium held in 1973[125] where the significance of the Church of the apostles for the contemporary Church was raised and discussed by ecumenically qualified theologians.

Of singular interest is John D. Zizioulas' study on the continuity of the theological conscience of the Orthodox Churches with the apostolic origin.[126] Zizioulas underscores as basic two of the many factors that have contributed to this continuity. The first is *Tradition* that plays a decisive role in forming the conscience of the Orthodox Churches. The second is the liturgy that attributes centrality and importance to worship in their lives and theology by developing a "theophanic" and "metahistorical" view of the Church. Although explicitly he has only the Orthodox Churches in mind while making this distinction, he is very much aware of its applicability to non-Orthodox Churches as well. We base the applicability of the study to ours on this all-inclusive nature of the distinction.[127]

The reader must understand that both these factors have historical roots. On the one hand, the apostles are presented to us in the biblical and patristic literature "as persons entrusted with a *mission* to fulfill. As such they are *sent* and thus *dispersed* in the world." From this point of view, they are understood as *individuals,* and they "represent a *link* between Christ and the Church and form part of a historical process with a decisive and perhaps *normative* role to play. Thus the idea of mission and that of historical process go together in the New Testament and lead to a scheme of continuity in a linear movement: God sends Christ—Christ sends the apostles—the apostles transmit the message of Christ by establishing Churches and Ministers. We may, therefore, call this approach 'historical.' "[128]

On the other hand, the apostles also have an *eschatological function*. In this regard, the apostles are understood as a *college* corresponding to the *eschata*. They "are not those who follow Christ but those who *surround* Him. And they do not stand as a link between Christ and the Church in a historical process but are the *foundations* of the Church in a presence of the Kingdom of God here and now."[129]

How is a synthesis of these two factors possible? Zizioulas gives a long and detailed answer to this question. However, for our purposes the following will suffice.

> The Apostles continue to speak and proclaim Christ in the Church only because the Church is by her very existence the living presence of the Word of God as person. Thus the Church, in listening to the word of the Apostles, listens as it were to her own voice, to the voice which comes from her very eschatological nature, echoing her own eschatological destiny. This makes the history of the Church identical with that of the world and of creation as a whole. Thus to recall that the Church is founded on the Apostles in an eschatological sense makes the Church acquire her ultimate existential significance as the sign of a redeemed and saved creation. This makes the Church, in the words of St. Paul, "the judge of the world," i.e., makes her acquire a prerogative strictly applied to the Apostles and especially to the Twelve in their eschatological function.[130]

This identification of the history of the Church with that of the world and of creation as a whole is a beautiful summation of what the human condition means if it is seen and judged in the light of the eschaton as the epicletic presence of the apostolic tradition.

> In an epicletical context, history ceases to be in itself a guarantee for security. The *epiclesis* means ecclesiologically that the Church *asks to receive from God what she has already received historically in Christ as if she had not received it at all,* i.e., as if history did not count in itself.... The epicletic life of the Church shows only one thing: That there is no security for her to be found in any historical guarantee as such—be it ministry or word or sacrament or even the historical Christ Himself. Her constant dependence on the Spirit proves that her history is to be constantly eschatological.[131]

The parish is the place where the Church, in hearing the Word of God and celebrating the Eucharist, receives what she has already received historically in Christ but anew as if she had not received it at all. Retrospection and eschatological vision are accomplished in it. History meets the future in the human condition experienced by those who receive the experiences of the apostolic Church, on the one hand, and the light of the eschatological Kingdom, on the other, to decipher and build the future. This is possible only if the Kingdom is already somehow present—or at least some of its features are already detectable—in man's reflection on the human condition in view of the Christian calling.

Any structure that can contribute to the understanding and the functioning of the creative tension of the past and the future, of history and eschatology, can and should be also considered as worthy of theological reflection. The parish is such a structure embracing history and pointing to the Kingdom in the concrete experiences of the Christians' human condition. In virtue of this duality, any effort toward working out models for the parish has a dual basis for reflection: revelation offering the Word of God and the Eucharist as an historical inheritance of the Christian community; and the human condition as the eschatological yearning for the full realization of the Kingdom of God here and now. Accordingly, the parish can be modeled as:

1) a community gathered together to hear the Word of God;
2) a community gathered together to celebrate the Eucharist;
3) a local organization of the universal Church;
4) a community restructured into small subcommunities;
5) the agent of change called for in the American experience.

The first two models are built on the data of revelation or history. The third and fourth stress elements of the human condition. The last is an interesting combination of both called for by the American experience and projecting a positive, creative approach to the future. The rest of our study will be devoted to the discussion of these models.[132]

CHAPTER III

THEOLOGICAL MODELS FOR THE PARISH

Meaning of the Term Model

In view of what has been said so far, it must be evident to the reader that there exist varied approaches to the concept and theology of the parish. The diverse views reflect specific theological personalities and their particular understanding and interpretation of the parish-reality, although some features—reduced to the minimum many times—remain the same in all of them. Because we believe that "the method of models or types . . . can have great value in helping people to get beyond the limitations of their own particular outlook, and to enter into fruitful conversation with others having a fundamentally different mentality,"[133] we feel that, by working out theological models for the parish, we are reaching out and actually creating a positive and constructive basis for imaginative reflection.

The term model is applied here in a twofold sense. First, it is an exemplar to be imitated since it is rooted and expressed, as the image of the ineffable, in biblical and patristic understanding of God's intervention in history and humanity's response to it manifest in religious practices. At the same time, model also signifies a pattern of something to be done, to operate, to be made. Consequently, a theological model has both historical and eschatological functions, i.e., the acceptance and approval of elements preserved from the past and the scrutiny and calling of the future. Only by possessing both these dimensions of the one and the same reality can it really be called a *theological* model in which revelation and the human condition are complementarily harmonized rather than set divisively against each other.[134]

1. The Parish Is a Community Gathered Together to Hear the Word of God

The Word of God in the Language of Man

The eternal God, hidden and incomprehensible, *revealed Himself in time* to the people of Israel. He thereby intervened in history and disclosed His merciful plans. The Bible (Word of God) is the record of this self-revelation of God which took place in a *message* as well as in *events* which this message announced and explained. God spoke and acted. The word and the event went together.

In thus revealing His face to man, God has also revealed to man his own human likeness. By making Himself man, God has brought it about that man has become the expression of the divine mystery. Although supernatural faith is needed to grasp what God wills to make known about Himself, it is only through man that the valid and authentic translation of this revelation can be effected.

> There was no need for God to make use of man in order to reveal Himself; but if He determined to do so, and did so by an in-humanization, then all the dimensions of human nature, known and unknown, are to be assumed and utilized to serve as means of expression for the absolute Person.[135]

Human language, the vehicle used by God, first of all *expresses human experience*. Man is essentially a *historic* being perfecting himself in time. He is led from childhood to adolescence, to maturity, to old age and no one of these stages is the assurance of another. Each human state entails the same looking forward as well as the attempt to retain at least in memory everything that has gone before and to incorporate it in our march forward. An experience in the present is true only to the extent that it is associated with a particular interpretation of the past and the future in the memory that guides us.

The truth of a living being is always contained in its whole reality—past, present, and future. Hence, the Word of God always includes the relationship between the past and the future. It creates history while establishing the truth in history:

> From a human point of view no text of secular litera-
> ture presents such a bewildering wealth of perspec-
> tives as does the Bible; one single word may have
> hundreds of echoes. The religious experiences of many
> ages are accumulated in such a word; and these un-
> wearying meditations, in responding to the immensity
> of the divine Word, have finally given to its human
> instrument a kind of corresponding infinity.[136]

God's revelation has respected this basic human experience of living in time. God speaks to man from within the
world, the starting-point of his own human experiences:

> Never has revelation fallen from heaven in order to
> communicate transcendent mysteries to man from
> without and from on high. God speaks to man from
> within the world, the starting point of his human ex-
> periences, penetrating His creatures so intimately
> that the divine *kenosis* was already announced in the
> Word of the Old Law and was no more than com-
> pleted in the incarnation.[137]

To speak signifies *to communicate freely one's innermost
being* to another by means of the perceptible sign of sounds.
This entails three elements: (a) the self-possession of a

spiritual person, present to himself, who knows and under-
stands his own *truth;* (b) perfect *freedom* to choose the
means of communication; and (c) a self-embracing and
self-determining quality, that is, one tending to *surpass sub-
jectivity* and go out toward another.

Hence, speech is an integral part of man's being. When
true, it manifests what being is. It participates in being
from its origin, illuminated from the beginning by the spirit;
and it thereby participates in the Word eternally pronounced in the heart of being by absolute Love. However,
human language is not yet characterized by truth, freedom,
and love. It must go beyond itself—toward its origin and
toward its goal. Man's speech emerges from his union with
material creation and is comprised of natural sounds and
gestures. Speech is also ordered to life; it wishes to act and
to create and entails commitment.

We might sum up as follows: (a) God speaks by man.
This means not only what man says but everything that he
is becomes God's instrument of communication. (b) The
particular Word of God which we call biblical revelation
necessarily transcends itself toward a word of all mankind
by referring itself back to creation and forward to the
coming of the Kingdom, the Day of Yahweh. (c) Since the
Word of God wills to unite itself with all mankind, nothing
human can be foreign to it. It makes use of every human
situation.

The Word of God in the Judeo-Christian Economy of Salvation

In the Judeo-Christian economy of salvation the Word
of God has always played an extraordinary and fundamental
role. In the *Old Testament,* it was the Word of creation
and the Word of the covenant that established the universe,
called the human race into existence, chose and held the
people of Israel together. It was the Word of God that,
after catastrophic lapses and infidelities, again and again
enabled the chosen people to regroup, to renew their cove-

nant, to rebuild Jerusalem and the temple, and to recreate the corporate-personality-idea of their belonging to one another, to Abraham, and to the living God.

Reading the Old Testament, one cannot but be astonished by the immense power of this Word of God particularly manifest in the diaspora-situation of the Jewish people and in their irradicable hope and conviction that the final fulfillment of God's promises to them must be fully realized. The history of the Israelites in Egypt, the self-revelation of God to Moses in the burning bush (Ex 3), and the covenant in the desert (Ex 16-31) are classical examples of the mysterious power of the Word of God. To hear it, Israel had to be called together (Dt 31:10-12; 2 K 23; Ne 8, 9, etc.). Listening to the Word led to an explanation of the Word (1 K 8:23; 2 K 8:9-10), then, to a profession of faith (Dt 27:14-26).

In the *New Testament*, the tone is set by Jesus' mission itself: "Let us go elsewhere to the neighboring country towns, so that I can preach there too because that is why I came" (Mk 1:38; cf. Lk 4:18-19). The Word of God, through Whom everything had its being, came to enlighten all men by becoming a Word to men (Jn 1). When He declared: "I tell you most solemnly, whoever listens to my words, and believes in the one who sent me" (Jn 5:24), He made the Word a medium of God's communication to man and of man's ascent to God (Jn 6:45).

Furthermore, He instructed the people continuously. He prepared the apostles and disciples for their future mission. He went from town to town and delivered the good news of salvation to all those who wanted to hear it. He also built His Church on Himself and on His Word: "If anyone loves me he will keep my word.... Those who do not love me do not keep my words. And my word is not my own: it is the word of the one who sent me. I have said these things to you while still with you; but the Advocate, the Holy Spirit, whom the Father will send in my name, will teach you everything and remind you of all I have said to you" (Jn 14:23-26).

We should also note that Jesus not only chose the Twelve as His helpers but also sent them out into the world with the instruction: "Go out to the whole world; proclaim the Good News to all creation" (Mk 16:16; cf. Mt 28:18). "Proclaim that the kingdom of heaven is close at hand" (Mt 10:7). "What I say to you in the dark, tell in the daylight; what you hear in whispers, proclaim from the housetops" (Mt 10:27). And the Acts of the Apostles is eloquent testimony to the wondrous working of the Word of God through the preaching of the apostles.

After receiving the Holy Spirit in the Upper Room, Peter immediately delivered a powerful address to the baffled crowd (Ac 2:14-36; cf. 3:12-26; 7:2-53; 10:34-43, etc.; consider also the many addresses delivered by Paul on his missionary journeys). The apostles were so conscious of their calling to deliver the Word of God that they did not hesitate to institute the ministry of the seven deacons for the service of the community and to free themselves for the ministry of the Word: "It would not be right for us to neglect the word of God. . . . We will continue to devote ourselves to prayer and to the service of the word" (Ac 6: 3-4).

The book of Acts also points out very clearly that the astounding success of the early Christian community was due to faithfulness to the teaching of the apostles, to faithfulness to the brotherhood created by the Word of God, to faithfulness to the breaking of bread, and to faithfulness to prayer for which daily they went to the temple where they also listened to the Old Testament and interpreted it in the light of their Christ-experience (2:42, 46).

The Word of God in the Life of the Christian

The Word of God is present and acts in the Church in many ways but especially in her *liturgical celebrations*. It is here that the Church realizes herself, becomes most completely what she is. And in this activity, Bible readings, biblical chants, and biblical commentary as well as the looser use of biblical formulas which pervades every rite, occupy such a permanent place that the liturgy has been rightly termed the "Bible in action."

The Christian liturgy has inherited from the synagogue the practice of reading a passage from the Sacred Scriptures at every assembly for prayer (Lk 4:16-21; Acts 13:27). However, it has given this action a new meaning: the risen Christ on the way to Emmaus before showing Himself in the breaking of the bread "interpreted what concerned Him in all the Scriptures" (Lk 24:27 and 31). He also told the apostles gathered together that everything written about Him "in the Law of Moses, the Prophets, and the Psalms had to be accomplished" (Lk 24:44). Accordingly, the Church has never ceased to have the texts of the Old Testament heard and also added to them the "teaching of the apostles" in which the early Christians were "assiduous" (Ac 2:42). Above all, she has added the very words of Jesus in the Gospel.

In the words of Vatican II: In the liturgy Christ "is present in His Word since it is He who speaks when the sacred Scriptures are read in the Church" and "in the liturgy God speaks to His people and Christ still proclaims His Gospel."[138]

The liturgical celebration reveals the mystery of the Word of God and gives it its highest degree of effectiveness. It is God who speaks and it is today that He addresses His people gathered together in response to His call. Thus, the liturgy gives the Bible its authentic interpretation. It also gives it its quality of present reality. And it indicates in a special way the passage from revelation to initiation in the faith.

The proclamation of the sacred text is followed by a commentary or homily. This is the adaptation of what has been read to the concrete circumstances of the moment and the needs of the present people. It is a pastoral act because it consists in breaking the bread of the word and a truly liturgical act since it is one with the readings whose efficacy it prolongs. In the Bible and in the liturgy there is an identical attitude before God, an identical vision of the world, and an identical interpretation of history. Hence, the liturgy proposes a living commentary of the Bible which gives it all its fullness of meaning.

> Through the typological exegesis of the liturgy, the Bible rediscovers its vitality and actuality. It ceases to be a simple story of the past in order to become my story: because it is a living mystery in whose dynamic current I am immersed. The promises of God to His people are promises made also to me; the prayer of the people of God becomes my prayer; the *wondrous works of God* accomplished by God in favor of His people are renewed on my behalf. In the sacramental liturgy I relive in brief the whole of sacred history, according to that great law of biology by which ontogenesis reproduces phylogenesis.[139]

It should also be noted that *Bible Vigils* or *Liturgies of the Word* are termed liturgical by some authors[140] and non-liturgical or paraliturgical by others.[141] However, regardless of their position on this subject, all authors agree[142] that in such celebrations Christ is present when the Word of God is read during such services. For we have the sign of the Word of God in the biblical text read and listened to; we have the reality of the reunion of the faithful in Christ's name; we are before the altar of God; and Christ speaks to us through the biblical word.[143]

> What is important to emphasize is that this presence of the Lord in the proclamation of His Word is not an analogical, figurative presence, as when in a cultural gathering one reads the works of a poet, entitling the reading: "Presence of that writer." It is a question here of a real and active presence of the Lord.[144]

This liturgical experience of the Scriptures is prolonged in *the everyday lives of the individual Christian* by private reading of the Bible. Reading the Word of God in faith is a divine encounter through which the word of pardon and redemption is extended to us. This encounter takes place in the Spirit. The Word is a sign containing what it announces.

Through Holy Scripture God addresses *us*. He speaks. We listen. The communication can be vital, penetrating, relevant. "For the Word of God is living and efficient and keener than any two-edged sword, and extending even to the division of soul and spirit, of joints also and of marrow" (Hb 4:12). . . . God instructs, demands and promises. Man learns, assents and accomplishes.[145]

The Second Vatican Council insisted that the faithful themselves must actively take in hand the reading and meditation of the Word of God:

This sacred Synod earnestly and specifically urges all the Christian faithful, too, especially religious, to learn by frequent reading of the divine Scriptures the "excelling knowledge of Jesus Christ" (Philippians 3:8). "For ignorance of the Scriptures is ignorance of Christ." Therefore, they should gladly put themselves in touch with the sacred text itself, whether it be through the liturgy, rich in the divine word, or through devotional reading, or through instructions suitable for the purpose and other aids which, in our time, are commendably available everywhere.[146]

The Word of God Creates a Community

"The people of God is gathered into one first of all through the Word of the living God."[147] The creative word of God uttered at the beginning of time and bringing forth the entire universe became the re-creating, regenerating Word of God in the process of salvation. Whenever it is proclaimed it can create a community and make it the carrier of the salvific proclamation. As in the first Christian community, in these new communities, too, Joel's prophecy can become an experiential reality: "Their sons and daughters shall prophesy" (Jl 3:1; cf. Ac 2:17), because "they were all filled with the Holy Spirit and began to proclaim the word of God boldly" (Ac 4:31). Not only the apostles, but the whole community, all those who had received the Spirit, were involved in the experience.

Paul was very much aware of the communal nature of the experience, and writing to the Corinthians, he was anxious to stress the point: "At all your meetings, let everyone be ready with a psalm or a sermon or a revelation, or ready to use his gift of tongues or to give an interpretation.... For you can all prophesy in turn, so that everybody will learn something and everybody will be encouraged" (1 Cor 14: 26, 31).[148] Floristan pointedly remarks in this regard:

> While the patristic age lasted, Christianity displayed an eminently missionary character owing to the heedfulness of the great bishops to the proclamation of the word of God and the maintenance of centers of catechumens.[149]

Although the mission of the apostles has always been clearly recognized and maintained in the Christian conscience preserving the historical dimension of Christianity, it is at least questionable whether the proclamation of the Kerygma and learning as a life-long characteristic of the Christian-catechumen have not been neglected and practically even denied in the modern and contemporary Church. If so, the Word of God has lost, to a great degree, its recreating and community-building quality. Certain features of the contemporary Church seem to indicate that this unfortunate situation is already an established fact.

The reader should think for a moment of the lack of thorough formation of the clergy in the biblical disciplines and of the embarrassing absence of biblical themes in preaching. Then, the precarious nature of catechetical instructions both in the Catholic school and in the CCD programs should be critically scrutinized. How unfortunate is it, too, that with Confirmation the whole learning process of the Christian as Christian comes to an end. Can we really be surprised, therefore, to find out that we are religious midgets rather than religious giants? That our conscience is practically formed without the Word of God playing its role in the process? And we are not even bothered by our professed ignorance in such a vital and important matter. We have so much faith in our own experiences that we keep forgetting or ignoring that even they must stand the judgment of the Word of God.

However, we must admit that there are signs—small, to be sure—that a change for the better is in the making. Under the impulsion of two great movements of the twentieth century—the liturgical movement and the biblical renewal —the Church is putting more and more stress on the Word of God. There has been a concerted effort to put fluent translations into the hands of the faithful in country after country with the accompanying exhortation to read the Word of God.

There has also been a diligent effort to incorporate much more of the Word of God in the liturgy. Working closely with exegetes of all nations, the Church has succeeded in publishing three important Lectionaries for worship (*Lectionary for Mass,* One-year cycle of Readings for the Liturgy of the Hours and Two-year cycle). She has also made profound use of the Word of God in each of the revised Sacramental Rites, strongly urging that the biblical texts be used whenever the Sacraments are administered. Unfortunately, the fact that such readings are available does not mean that they will be used to the full or even at all.

A word of caution is in place here, however. Though we stress the importance of receiving the Word of God, we do not understand it merely as an historical deposit that has to be received and preserved intact. On the contrary, what is handed over to us has to respond to the human condition and exercise its eschatological function; consequently, it has to be delivered to us anew. To quote Zizioulas again,

> The apostolic kerygma needs to be constantly placed in the Spirit in order to be life and not just words. It cannot be an objectified norm in itself, something that judges the community of the Church from above and from outside. It is in the context of the *koinonia* of the Spirit, which implies the concrete continuity of the Church, that the kerygma of the Apostles can be "continued" in a living way.[150]

The return to the biblical and patristic understanding of the function of the Word of God in the forming of faith-communities, has generated new efforts toward bringing it back to the contemporary Church as one of the most power-ful—and also, perhaps, most neglected—forces revitalizing Christian communities. We intend to present here only two such efforts, one from Central and the other from South America. Though the technical aspects of working out these realizations of the model are closely connected with and rooted in the particular situation and atmosphere of the places involved, the amazing results are indications of possi-ble similar accomplishments wherever the Word of God be-comes a constitutive element of the Christian community.

The San Miguelito Experiment

Three American priests from Chicago started an experi-ment in the parish of Cristo Redentor, better known as San Miguelito, on the edge of Panama City, March, 1963.[151] The main problem faced by the priests and interested lay people was how to develop a living parish that would be aware of both the historical and the eschatological dimensions of its very nature. They envisaged a parish that would remain faithful to the apostolic tradition and at the same time would be "dynamically related to the world that is emerging in the rapidly changing neighborhoods of Panama City." Fr. Leo Mahon, the leader, and his associates knew very well that they had to reach out for "some new expression of the life of Christ in the lives of men," theologically as well as sociologically, to find a truly Christian answer to the problem. In view of the sociological aspect, they chose the San Miguelito geographical area with a poor but reasonably stable population and with good possibilities for growing into a community. The theological aspect has been concisely set forth by Joseph Fitzpatrick, S.J.:

> Three basic principles guided the experiment: (1) the need to form a living Christian community (the family of God); (2) the need to form the Christian community by the Word of God (the Scriptures); and (3) prophecy, the spiritual gift by which priest or layman becomes sensitive to the meaning of the Word of God for the community, and sensitive to the ways in which the Spirit of God is seeking to express itself in the community.[152]

The reader should realize that these three principles involved a rather revolutionary approach to the whole idea of the parish in 1963. The aim was not, Fitzpatrick points out, to build a large church or to create a routine of religious services or even to build a parochial school. Neither did the priests intend to judge the result of their work by the sheer number of baptisms or by figures for attendance at Mass. "The major thrust was the effort to find community where it existed, to foster its development where it did not exist. and to form it spiritually and religiously."[153]

What kind of method did they use to attain their objective? It can be described in four steps.

Step one. The priests searched for families and lay leaders as well as for neighborhood situations, natural communities particularly suited for development. They were looking for married couples, and—since they were in Central America—for men, but never for women alone or children. After having found them, with the help of lay leaders they called neighborhood meetings. These meetings were devoted not to discussing Mass, sacraments, or attendance at church but to the problems of the neighborhoods which priests and people sought together to solve with the help of the principles of Christian family life and community. If the conditions were found favorable, these preparatory neighborhood meetings lasted for ten weeks.[154]

Step two. Able and interested people were invited to make a cursillo, not "to achieve personal conversion, but rather to provide more intensive formation in the theological and scriptural basis of the Christian community." Interestingly, salvation was presented to them as the reunion of the dispersed people of God in the Hebrew experience.

Step three. The neigborhood meetings and the intensive study broke the ground for joyful community celebrations, held not in cathedrals or large churches but in small chapels, homes, and buildings scattered all over the parish. A large parish center was also available for meetings, occasionally for Mass and for other religious gatherings. It is, however, important to bear in mind that the traditional and the eschatological elements always left their mark on the celebrations. Fitzpatrick describes them thus:

> The resurrection, the hope and joy of a people who share a life already risen in Christ, are explained as the base on which the Christian community must live, with eyes on the eventual fulfillment of the perfect family of God in the parousia. This comes as a sharp and direct challenge to a Latin culture in which preoccupation with death has dominated Christian life; in which Good Friday, not Easter Sunday, has been the sacred day of the year; and in which a sense of sin has been a heavy burden often over-powering a sense of personal worth. When one observes the reaction and response of simple people to this message, one can feel the strong impact of the "good news." One senses their reaction to the word of God: *No man has ever spoken to us as this man has.*[155]

Step four. To make the movement lasting, extensive, effective, and future-oriented, an informed and qualified lay leadership had to be provided. The prospective leaders were selected from their own neighborhoods, shared the experiences of the people they lived with, and after a good and intensive training in leadership were sent back to them. The training was designed to enable the leaders to communicate experiences effectively. In other words, they were expected to translate into concrete expression *their* own experience of the human condition. How could they do so? By learning to reflect on them, first of all, in the light of the Word of God. Therefore, "for five hours each day the participants gather for a common, meditative reading of the Scriptures, for an exchange of ideas about the meaning of the passages read, in an effort to gain the beginning of insight, of vision."[156]

It must have been an indescribably re-awakening experience for these spiritually gifted participants actually to recognize in biblical passages their own personal and community problems, and to see revelation and the human condition play mutually complementary roles in understanding themselves and their communities. They emerged from their training in leadership as people charged with a prophetic role: to receive the Word actively, i.e., to study and interpret it as a true medium for understanding the experiences of the people of their own times and places. To quote Fitzpatrick once more:

> Thus there is a constant interplay of community, Scripture and prophet. This is not a vague grasping of new doctrine; it all takes place within the doctrinal framework of the Church. It is rather an effort to relate doctrine to experience, a constant and intensive searching for the meaning of the Word of God for this community.[157]

Such a model could certainly not be considered traditional, if it is measured against the way the parish has developed since the Middle Ages. It is, however, very traditional if it is interpreted according to biblical and patristic trends, for it brings back the powerful quality of the Word of God in creating communities as effective signs of God's saving presence in the human condition. The leaders of such a radically Christian trend "know the community intimately, they know what things mean to it, they have a feel for the fundamental realities of life and they grasp immediately the significance of the Scriptures for the community, as a professionally trained priest from outside the community never could. They have an openness that the priests evidently find it difficult to achieve."[158] Perhaps, the people of San Miguelito are right when they claim that priests are afraid of the Word of God.

The Segundo-Experience

The Word of God has also played a predominant part in another contemporary effort toward the renewal of the Church, an effort undertaken by Juan Luis Segundo, S.J. and his pastoral team. Methodologically, they decided to do two things: (1) to consult with hundreds of lay people to identify the problems of living the Christian faith today, and (2) to work out *with them* the implications of faith for life.[159]

The immediate purpose of their studies and discussions was not, therefore, to form a particular parish community, as was the case of San Miguelito. They wished rather to understand and spell out some important factors that have already entered into the mind of the contemporary man but either have never been integrated into the Christian consciousness or, if they have been somehow integrated, have not yet fully yielded the conclusions that flow logically from them. Hence, the primary thrust of the whole enterprise was more theological than organizational, in spite of the fact that the circumstances in which these studies and discussions have begun and are being continued have been less than theological in the technical sense of the term.

In the background of the whole project lies a twofold crisis. On the one hand, Christians are experiencing today the painful process of losing their faith. Not because they want to, but because "it would seem that among many Christians the process of growing into mature human beings is estranging them from the faith."[160] On the other hand, even the faithful Christian experiences almost insurmountable problems in trying to cope with doctrinal trends and interpretations resulting from acceleration as a permanent constitutive element of contemporary life and experience.

For when the Christian faith "is expressed in a language different from that of today, our contemporaries find it alien to them; it is a quaint museum piece. Those who 'have the faith' often see it as something that *should be* the most dynamic and meaningful thing for living in today's world. But in fact it is not. All too often it has been transformed into a hideout for people who dare not or cannot live the adventure of *being a human being today.*"[161]

In this citation are the two factors that must enter into any effort toward a theological understanding of the people of God in the parish: the demands of faith and those of being truly human, the same two elements that inspired the people involved in the San Miguelito experiment. Yet the starting points are greatly different from each other. While the leaders of San Miguelito started their approach to the parish with reflection on the Word of God, the Segundo-people opted for the human condition as their springboard.

> This type of theology essentially starts with, and takes account of, the world in which our contemporaries live and work. To be sure, it works in close collaboration with its specialized sister theology—note that we do not call her "big sister"—but it retains its own proper and inalienable personality in the task of transmitting the faith.[162]

Surprisingly, however, the conclusion is drawn in the light of revelation. Human experience and the human condition must withstand the last judgment so powerfully presented in Matthew's gospel (25:31-46). If one reflects very carefully on both the reward and the rejection as well as on the surprise of both the rewarded and the rejected, one must come to the conclusion, Segundo claims, that the Christian is a believer because he has accepted revelation which will culminate in the last judgment as the light and the judge of the human condition. He can, therefore, claim that "the Christian is he *who already knows.* This, undoubtedly, is what distinguishes and defines him."

Let us put this in more general terms. Through Christ, God gave every man the possibility of loving others, and he joined all men and every individual in solidarity; he thus put love in everyone's hands as the divine instrument of salvation. This possibility is as vast and as ancient as humanity itself. It does not date from A.D. 1 or 30. Nor is it limited by the historical limits of the ecclesial community. Through Christ, it reaches all men. The more traditional strains of theology have always echoed these perspectives: The redemptive work of Christ, carried out within history, goes beyond the limits of time and dominates the whole unfolding development of the universe—both its past and its future.

But there is something that begins with Christ and that moves out solely toward the future: namely, the revelation of this plan that suffuses all time. The Christian is not the only one to enter into this plan. But he is the one who knows it. He knows the plan because he has received not only redemption but also revelation.

The Christian is *he who knows.* Does this definition give us the key we need to unite and synthesize the universal perspective of salvation with the foundation of a particular community called the Church in the framework of history? That is what we shall try to see in the following chapters.[163]

The Christian who already knows is, therefore, a witness to revelation as the guiding light in deciphering, evaluating, and answering the mysteries of the human condition. The Word of God has such a unique function in his life that it cannot be replaced by anything.

How does this apply to the parish-community? The Church can be described as both "the community of faith and the sacraments" and "the community of believers, that is, of those who have faith in what God has revealed."[164] Consequently, the Christian, living in and being a part of a faith-community, is in a position of knowing and called upon to share his knowledge with his fellowmen for the benefit of mankind.

> We can conclude that revelation is both a revelation of God and of what is happening with the human race. Saint Paul indeed describes Christian revelation as knowledge of the *mystery*. And for him, mystery signifies a divine plan, hidden but universal in its operation, that runs throughout history. This plan of love, centered around the historical Incarnation and redemptive work of Christ, has two planes as it were. On one plane, the Incarnation and Redemption operate from the beginning of humanity to its end. On the other plane, *knowledge* of this loving plan operating as mystery in the Incarnation and Redemption is at work solely from the time Christ came into human history.[165]

If one can accept this conclusion, one also realizes that the Christian does not possess the Word of God for his own sake. On the contrary, he has been chosen as a carrier and a deliverer. This function is always exercised on the local level, where people gather together to hear the Word of God as a conscience-forming agent. It has to penetrate human conscience. It has to ferment and transform it. This process of transformation will then give rise to a community that can become a conscience-forming agent itself.

Thanks to the wisdom of which Saint Paul speaks, the Church is the consciousness of humanity as it were. She is humanity arriving at full awareness of what is taking place in it. Thus, as we have already seen, the Church is all humanity in a certain sense. She is the congregation of the human race, just as that which is conscious in us represents our whole being.[166]

What is, then, our conclusion? The Word of God is a powerful factor in creating faith-communities. The parish either thrives on it or merely stagnates and slowly dies. Yet the Word of God has to be received always as a response to the human condition. Otherwise it "is constantly in danger of becoming mere words.... This signifies that revealed truth itself is seeking its incarnation in the final truth, the truth of everyday human activity which prompts and demands dialogue."[167] It is on the parish-level that the realization of such a fundamental understanding of Christianity must find its concrete forms. The people gathered together to hear the Word of God might take different forms in different places and at different times. Hearing the Word and responding to it, however, remains a constant in every form in all places and at all times. Without it the very being of the parish-community would actually be destroyed.

2) The Parish Is a Community Gathered Together To Celebrate the Eucharist

Liturgy Is Man's Response to God's Word

God desires that the Word He speaks to men should be effective; it awaits a response. But the response is that which God Himself has willed: it is still His Word. This mystery is realized fully in the Person of Jesus. He is the Prophet on whom the Spirit rests, the Messiah, the Word-made-flesh; as such He announces to the world in human words the Good News of God's saving plan of love. He is also the sovereign priest who offers to the Father the sacrifice of thanksgiving: in His death the homage of total obedience and in His resurrection the praise of a new and holy race of men. The work of Christ is the perfect speech of God in the world restored and realized by Christ.

The liturgy, as Pope Pius XII declared in *Mediator Dei*, "is nothing more or less than the exercise of Christ's priestly function"; in the liturgy the priesthood of Christ becomes "a continuing and living reality in all ages until the end of time" (no. 22). In other words, the liturgy is the public worship which our Redeemer as Head of the Church renders to the Father as well as the worship which the community of the faithful renders to its Founder, and through Him to the Father.

Thus, the core of the liturgy is the Paschal Mystery whose content is nicely summarized by L. Bouyer:

> It is the re-enactment in, by, and for the Church of the act of Our Lord which accomplished our salvation, that is, his passion and death in the fullness of their final effects—the resurrection, the communication of savage grace to mankind, and the final consummation of all things.[168]

Therefore, the Bible and the liturgy signify the two terms of the divine-human dialogue: at the point of departure is the inspired Word; at the goal, the sacrament of unity. The two great signs or sacraments used in the liturgy are: (1) the sacrament of the Word, which is Scripture, and (2) the Sacrament of the Deed, which refers to the acts of Christ made present to us in sacred symbol. Both are of equal importance and must work together if God is to speak to us and we are to answer.

The liturgy can be celebrated validly and in many cases even legitimately without an assembly. However, its celebration calls for the gathering of the faithful, presupposes that this is realized, and must therefore provoke it by eliciting the necessary pastoral effort.

> Liturgical services are not private functions, but are celebrations of the Church, which is the "sacrament of unity," namely, a holy people united and organized under their bishops.... Whenever rites, according to their specific nature, make provision for communal celebration involving the presence and active participation of the faithful, this way of celebrating them is to be preferred, as far as possible, to a celebration that is individual and quasi-private.[169]

The liturgical assembly is acknowledged to be the most expressive manifestation of the Church. There are, indeed, other visible expressions of it, notably General Councils, pilgrimages to Rome, instructions given by pastors outside the assembly, the charitable services of the community, and above all the sending forth of missionaries to non-believers. But out of them all the liturgical assembly constitutes the most common, ordinary, and accessible manifestation of the Church.

No sacred action shows us more clearly how the Church responds to God with His own Word than the summit of the liturgy, that is, the Eucharist. It is the expression of a dialogue between God and His Church.

The Centrality of the Eucharist in the Church

In the words of Vatican II: "At the Last Supper, on the night when He was betrayed, our Savior instituted the Eucharistic Sacrifice of His Body and Blood. He did this in order to perpetuate the sacrifice of the Cross throughout the centuries until He should come again, and so to entrust to His beloved spouse, the Church, a memorial of His death and resurrection."[170] The Church desires that the faithful should participate knowingly, devoutly, and actively in this rite, be instructed by God's Word and be refreshed at the table of the Lord's body.

We find reaffirmed culturally herein the great principle which is a melodic theme of the divine symphony of the history of salvation: the initiative is always on God's part Who continues to address His Word to man and awaits a response of love from him. On the one hand, the Eucharistic liturgy reveals the whole ineffable reality of its mystery by relating itself through the Word to the historical development of God's plan; on the other hand, the liturgy of the Word does not disappear in a hazy and detached memorial of distant things but takes hold of them all and makes them live in the sacramental present of the Eucharist.

The union of these two parts in a single celebration merely represents sacramentally the unitary development of the mystery of salvation: from the Word that God pronounces and man hears, to the Word made flesh and "awaited" among us.[171] Thus wherever the Word of God is taken to heart, the Eucharistic celebration naturally follows.

When we explore beneath the surface, we find that the whole liturgic life of Christendom is built on a double foundation: the Bible and the Eucharist. The uttered Word and the living Presence, the holy doctrine and the holy food, the message of salvation and the sacrifice of praise, are the gathering points of devotion wherever Christian worship retains and expresses its real character, as a loving and grateful response of the creature to the self-revelation and self-giving of God.... Both types of worship are plainly needed if the whole mind of the Church—ethical and mystical, practical and other-worldly—is to be expressed; and justice is to be done to her dual nature, so profoundly historical, yet so profoundly supernatural too.[172]

We have already seen in the San Miguelito experiment

that a tremendous appreciation of and expectation for the Eucharist grew out of the spiritual formation of the people by the Word of God, not as an isolated experience of individual piety, but as a banquet of God's family, as "the sacrament of the unifying love of the Christian community."[173]

The documents of Vatican II, quoted earlier, have also defined the parish in its Eucharistic role and function, indicating the Eucharist's centrality in the life of the Christian community. The Council fathers felt so strongly about it that they did not hesitate to state clearly and unmistakably that "no Christian community . . . can be built up unless it has its basis and center in the celebration of the most Holy Eucharist."[174]

The Communal Nature of the Eucharist

The primitive Church was strong and invincible because its members remained faithful "to the breaking of the bread" in addition to being faithful to the apostles, to the brotherhood, and to prayers (Ac 2:42, 46; cf. 20:7). It can be said, therefore, that, according to the testimony of history, the Eucharist has marked the Church's life so deeply and so essentially since the very first moment of her existence that it has always been understood as both the source and the sign of the Christian's union with Christ and with one another as a community.

This is the fact that the experience of the Eucharist was always a communitarian experience. The paradigm around which the theological reflection of the Fathers of Christian teaching centered was the celebration of the Eucharist by the whole of the Christian community in a given city or parish. Indeed, the emphasis on the unity of the community celebrating the Eucharist was so strong that only one celebration was permitted on each altar and only one altar was permitted in each church. It was only in the 5th century that it became acceptable to celebrate another Mass for those who could not be present at the Eucharist of the bishop, indeed even to celebrate at the bishop's altar. But even here, the basic consideration was the fact that not everyone could fit into the bishop's church for the bishop's Eucharist. Thus, the image of the Eucharist which formed the basis of theological reflection was one of the Eucharist celebrated by the entire Christian community assembled together around the bishop who, in turn, was surrounded by his choir of priests. The bishop celebrated the Eucharist, but the community was seen as concelebrating with him, each according to his rank in the community, deacons and priests assisting at the altar as needed, the congregation joining the choir in antiphonal chants and processional hymns, but all celebrating the one Eucharist.

Thus, the primary emphasis in the theology of the Eucharist from the beginning was the fact that the Eucharist is the image and source of the unity of the Christian community.[175]

At least this is what the Church experienced everywhere up to the sixth century. It was always the local community that celebrated, in union with the universal Church, the believers' sacramental union with Christ and with one another. This is why all prayers were recited by the entire celebrating community. The Scripture passages were not just read, they were *proclaimed* to the community, and all present *listened* hoping to be inspired by the Word of God that prepared them for the Eucharistic consummation of their communal union with the Lord. Therefore, all those present received communion. The Eucharist was the community, the here-and-now actualization of the personal presence of the Lord in their midst.

It is really unfortunate and regrettable that as a result of many factors, particularly the use of the Latin language that had become foreign to the common people, this communal celebrating character of the Eucharistic gathering simply got lost in history after the sixth century,[176] at a time when country-parishes became more and more numerous, and needed the cohesive, community-forming element of the Eucharist. Instead, it was turned into an object of private devotion of the priest and the *mysterium tremendum* that frightened the people away from the altar. At least in the West, this development meant tragedy for the Church. For, while for the first five centuries the parish knew only one model for the believing local community, a combination of the celebration of the Word of God and of the Eucharist, with the transformation of the Eucharistic doctrine into a silent performance by the priest, whispering particularly the canon as if it had nothing to do with the people, even this one model could not fully function. It is no wonder, then, that the people turned to recitation of private prayers instead of participating actively in the celebration.

This lamentable situation became only further aggravated by the lack of education of the priests, by the poverty of preaching, and by the fact that many parishes were owned by nobles and monasteries, etc. The result of these developments was the complete loss of the sense of community.

> Previous ages had experienced and understood the Eucharist as the celebration and daily nourishment of the unity of the community of the Church in the body of Christ. Medieval piety, on the other hand, considered the Eucharist as the possession of the priest and defined his priesthood in terms of the power to consecrate.[177]

Unfortunately, the Church had to wait until well into the nineteenth century for an effort toward bringing back the communitarian aspect of the breaking of the bread, and for stressing again the parish as a gathering for listening to the Word of God and for celebrating the Eucharist. The

Tübingen school was responsible for this new theological orientation by returning to the biblical and patristic sources for inspiration and interpretation. The liturgical and ecumenical movements have also contributed greatly to a deeper interest and involvement in the celebration of the Eucharist. It is, therefore, not by accident that, starting with A. Wintersig in 1925, theologians began to pay greater attention to the parish as a Eucharistic community. Pius XII's *Mediator Dei*, in 1947, and Paul VI's *Mysterium Fidei*, in 1965, were helpful means in stressing the Eucharistic aspect of Christian life.

> It is the public worship of the Church, the act in which the Church gathers together before God in Christ, acknowledging the fact that her existence as God's people is God's own and constant gift. As true worship, it must express the daily life which the Church leads as a community to be true. And, at the same time, it is the action in which, precisely because it is the symbolic self-expression of the deepest reality of the Church (that she is one in Christ), the Church grows as Church.[178]

The Eucharist and the Human Condition

This slow but interesting development of Eucharistic theology from the viewpoint of the parish, aided greatly by the light of ecumenical dialogue, found the synthesis of the historical and the eschatological, of revelation and the human condition, in the Eucharist itself. Therein tradition (1 Cor 11:23-25; Lk 22:19), the recalling of what the Lord did, stresses powerfully, in the very words of the Lord, the given, the historical fact.

> As such it activates the historical consciousness of the Church in a retrospective way. At the same time, however, the Eucharist is the eschatological moment of the Church *par excellence*, a remembrance in the

Kingdom, as it sets the scene for the convocation of the dispersed people of God from the ends of the earth in one place, uniting the 'many' in the 'one' and offering the taste of the eternal life of God here and now. In and through the same experience, therefore, *at one and the same moment*, the Church unites in the Eucharist the two dimensions, past and future, simultaneously as one indivisible reality. This happens 'sacramentally,' i.e., in and through historical and material forms, while the existential tension between the 'already' and the 'not yet' is preserved.[179]

This synthesis of history and eschatology, of revelation and the human condition, makes the people of God gathered together for the celebration of the Eucharist a perfect model of the parish. At least in theory. Does it work in practice? Is it conceivable that even today, with a slowly but surely dwindling Church attendance, the celebration of the Eucharist still can and should be considered as the unifying center and high point of the life of the parishioners? Can we claim with Cyprian Vagaggini that "one of the best means of making the priests and the people in our day appreciate once more the essentially communitarian and sacral nature of the Church is to begin by making them rediscover all the wealth of meaning of the *ecclesia* as liturgical assembly"?[180]

Statistics certainly go against such a claim. Yet the model is not only valid; it is needed more than ever to revitalize the Church. The question is, therefore, not whether it could or should be done, but rather how it should be done.

Much has been written about this problem in our century. Practically, the whole liturgical movement owes its existence to it. A medieval development, harmful to the communitarian understanding of the liturgy in general and of the Eucharist in particular, has become the springboard for the promoters of the liturgy. We are thinking of the specifically Western development of the private "votive

Masses," with us since the sixth century, that gave way later on to the so-called "low Masses." Interestingly, the liturgical movement concentrated all its efforts on the latter because the low Masses were the only ones where a dialogue could be introduced and a lay leader used. The purpose of the whole movement has been to restore the communal character of the Eucharistic celebration to the parish by restoring the Mass to the people. J. A. Jungmann remarks very perceptively in this regard:

> From what has been said one will gather that so far we have done little more than lurch from one make-shift to the next. It will be for the reform initiated by the Second Vatican Council to devise a congregational Mass that is both correct in its form and meaningful to the men of our time.[181]

Here we have again a reference to the two basic factors of Christianity: the correct form of the Eucharistic celebration which is in line with history, and its meaningfulness to the men of our time which is in line with the human condition prevalent in modern man's conscience. When Jungmann refers to the present, he has in mind the universal Church becoming visible in the local Eucharistic gathering; the here and now of God's sacramental presence, the sharing of the Lord at the banquet-table where His body and blood are offered to all who care to partake of them.[182]

As the Word of God reached its apex in the Incarnation, so partaking of the presence of the Lord culminates in the Eucharistic banquet. And as the Word of God was always given for the benefit of mankind through the understanding and interpretation of the people of God, so the Eucharistic sacrifice recalls and re-creates the one sacrifice of the Lord through its celebration by a parish-community for the benefit of the universal Church and the good of mankind. This unifying character of the Eucharist is the greatest response to man's continuous craving to eliminate factionalism from his ranks and to reunite all men in seeking their common good in a universal brotherhood of men.

The Eucharist and Parochial and Subparochial Communities

How can the reform initiated by Vatican II respond to this need of making the Eucharist once again a unifying power and a community-creating-force for the contemporary Christians?

First, we have to create a Eucharistic consciousness in every parish community. Vatican II laid down the foundation of such an understanding of and doctrinal approach to the parish by spelling out clearly the bishop's unparalleled role and the Eucharist's centrality. The former is "the visible principle and foundation of unity in his particular church"; he also "represents his own church," and together with all the bishops, in union with the Pope, "the entire Church joined in the bond of peace, love, and unity."[183] Why is the bishop so prominent in the diocese and the universal Church? The Council gives a very simple answer to this question:

> A bishop, marked with the fullness of the sacrament of orders, is "the steward of the grace of the supreme priesthood," especially in the Eucharist, which he offers or causes to be offered, and by which the Church constantly lives and grows.[184]

It is the bishop who offers the Eucharist or causes it to be offered. And the Eucharist is the real, most powerful bond among Christians and Christian communions, to such an extent that they can and do form one supernatural unity among themselves and with the Lord as His Mystical Body.

In order to achieve a Eucharistic consciousness in the parish, catechesis must concentrate on this communitarian character and purpose of the Eucharistic celebration. Private piety should give precedence to the role and function of the community. What is the particular purpose of celebrating the Eucharist in this locally designated community, at this determined time of history?—this should be the leading question in the minds of all those, priests and people, who get together in remembering the Lord. How can this local community grow in awareness of belonging to the Lord and to one another and of being the concrete realization of all those who are equally members of the Lord's Body? And how should this particular community avail itself of the influence of Eucharistic conviction and faith in developing responsibilities toward the greater human community as such? The study and application of the Orthodox Church's Eucharistic ecclesiology could be more than helpful on this point.[185]

Second, the post-Vatican parish communities should be allowed to experiment with different ways of making the Eucharistic celebration more communitarian in form and more experiential by personal and community involvement. Can it be done today?

Andrew M. Greeley's article, "The New Community," in *The Critic*, 1966, could be considered a pace-setter on the American scene in spite of the fact that Greeley was not the first one to propose the subcommunity idea for urban parishes.[186]

His initial thesis is the following. "The secret of establishing a parish community is to find out what are the natural communities which exist within the territory of the parish and bring the parish to each of these natural communities while at the same time providing through the parish a structure in which the various natural communities can relate to one another."[187]

Interestingly, our Protestant brethren must have shared our own disappointing experiences in regard to declining interest in the Eucharistic celebration, for some five years later, Urban T. Holmes III wrote in characteristically similar terms:

We need to reconstitute our church life into small groups (more than fifty begins to get cumbersome) after the sect model, which in turn are 'cells' of a large church (constituting maybe two or three thousand members or more). The sects would meet in some multipurpose building for the liturgy, including preaching, and would identify themselves in terms of the sacramental person who presides at their gatherings. Both the rite and preaching would be of the informal, interpersonal character. Pastoral care and administration would be either of a very *light* variety or simply referred back to the 'mother church.'[188]

These references seem to indicate that the failure of modern big-city parishes is attributable to the lack of vision on the part of ecclesiastical people to work with the natural subgroups within their boundaries and to the lack of appreciation for decentralized liturgy and spiritual activities. In saying this, however, we must stress that neither of the writers quoted above is asking for the suppression of the parochial principle. On the contrary, both propose it as a much needed center to coordinate periodically the natural subcommunities. As a matter of fact, Greeley states very clearly:

There seems to be emerging a 'new community' sometimes subparochial and sometimes transparochial and never antiparochial which has some interesting and perhaps important implications for future developments within the Church.[189]

In another article on the parish, he is more specific on the function of the parish and on its relationship with the natural subcommunities by describing the parish "as basically a formational and liturgical center," and by claiming that this is exactly the viewpoint that should prevail in judging "the benefit and relevance of a given form of primary group experience on the parochial level."[190] Therefore, he maintains that some form of the parish is necessary for the Church to function properly for the simple reason that "for most Catholics, during most of their lives, the parish is the only place where they are in formal contact with the Church."[191]

At the same time, he makes it very clear that "the parish can no longer be relied upon as the only or even the major level at which the Church is engaged. The pious legend that the parish priest is the only priest really on the front lines should be forever put to rest."[192] But it can be relied upon as basically a formational and liturgical center, modeled as a community gathered together to hear the Word of God and to celebrate the Eucharist, provided that it is built on some kind of natural community or natural subcommunities. These subcommunities are not ends in themselves, as the parish is not an end in itself either. Their function is initiatory, preparatory, and conditioning. They have to open up to the needs of the Church as such and to all genuine human needs.

> The new community is a series of relationships where individuals get the support and strength they need for Christian commitment in all the other areas of human endeavor. It replaces nothing but merely adds another dimension to the life of its members. It is a fellowship where the deepest of values are reinforced; it is a group where old ideas are revived and new ideas are obtained. It is a place where one can relax and be one's self because one senses that one is loved. It is a community where one may worship consciously and explicitly as a member of the community. It is a retreat where one may obtain perspective, stimulation, courage and encouragement. It is a fellowship where one is convinced once again that interest in and dedication to the work of the Church are not silly or foolhardy or optional.[193]

Michael M. Winter, whose theological vision of the parish

we will treat more in detail later on in this work, adds another dimension to the justification of the sub- or primary communities, i.e., the ancient conviction that, normally, community and celebration coincide, and so "the normal setting for Mass ought to be among the acknowledged members of the basic Christian community," namely, as in the first generation of Christianity, "the house Mass of a small group must be the normal pattern of liturgical worship."[194] He also remarks that only if small domestic groups are made into fundamental Eucharistic communities, can we really hope to promote the feeling of responsibility in the lay members of the parish. And if and when this takes place the Eucharist as source and cause of unity within the primary group becomes a proven fact.

The Power of the Eucharist Rightly Celebrated

What have we, then, discovered in this analysis? Two things have become evident to us in our course of reflection on the second model of the parish. First, that even such an exalted mystery as the Eucharist demands and supposes as its underlying element the recognition of the human in sub- or primary communities. Without this the unity of the partakers of the Eucharist can hardly be achieved. Second, wherever the sub- or primary communities are present and taken seriously, the Eucharist, historically treasured by Christianity, can do what nothing else can, i.e., mold them into a spiritual and, to some extent, even social union on the level of the community that is stronger than blood relation. Understanding the human condition in the common ideals and concerns, and strengthening it in the reality of God's love, man finds the best possible and most powerful medium in the Eucharist for his search of unity and peace.

Admittedly, there is never a time in most parishes when all parishioners can assemble for a single Eucharist and thus present the spectacle of a complete parish gathered around its pastor, the representative of the bishop. Modern circumstances usually compel the celebration of successive Eucharistic celebrations in which only a part of the parish can participate at one time. Yet these different congregations gathered around associate pastors represent the whole parish in much the same way as the different parishes represent the diocese and the dioceses represent the entire Church.

In order that the parishioners who come together may truly represent the Church, however, their assembly must have a quality essential to the Church—a hierarchical structure of persons differing in rank and function. The distribution of liturgical roles signifies that the assembly is not a haphazard gathering of people but a manifestation of the Church.

Since the Eucharist is a covenant-sacrifice, when the community celebrates it each member enters anew into the covenant, making it his own. In this way, he exercises the share in the priesthood of Christ—whether general or ministerial—that has been conferred on him by baptism and ordination. It is the repetition of this action of the Church in many places and especially in parishes which builds up the Church and keeps her in being.

> The Eucharist reveals the nature of the Church, and in each celebration of particular communities the Church continues to discover afresh the dynamic source of its structure and the ultimate meaning and purpose of all its activity. Without the Church there can be no Eucharist, but without the Eucharist there would be no Church—each stands as a sign of the other.[195]

In an address at the "Priest in the Modern World Forum" of the University of Loyola in Chicago, in January, 1965, Fr. Leo T. Mahon, the leader of the San Miguelito priests-group, made an interesting twofold distinction between teaching Christian doctrine and preaching the Word of God, on the one hand, and community organization and the making of the Church, on the other.[196] Though he did not develop the second part of the distinction in the address, he returned to it in an essay included in Report No. 13. The following powerful statement is found there:

> The call to Christianity, then, is the call to greatness, the call to become the most human, the most holy, the most divine of all peoples and, by so being, provide the impetus and example to all our brothers to respond to the Word they hear in their nature. Thus we preach a very special vocation to the people—to be a great people, to be a sign and the light for all the rest.[197]

The process of becoming the most human, a sign and the light for all the rest, culminates in the sacramental-liturgical activity of the celebrating local community when, as their first and foremost task as a Christian community, they become the actual concretization of the Church. How true it is that

> in the Eucharist . . . the liturgy reaches its human-divine climax. We begin by confessing our division and guilt, and begging pardon; the ministers of the Word once more issue the call to freedom, the challenge to be the people of God; then the president of the assembly thanks God for being His people and thrills the assembly by sounding the call to action: "Let us be His people, let us be one," and by means of the Sacred fraternal meal the assembly more than ever becomes the people of God—with and in the Lord, one in love, and pardon, hope and sacrifice. Thus in one solemn moment, the whole of salvation history is reenacted, the paschal mystery of the Lord renewed, the Church is formally made present; in one great moment is lived in anticipation the ultimate destiny of man: perfect love and union.[198]

Reading lines like these can delight the believers' hearts and can provoke mocking or sarcastic remarks on the part of doubters and unbelievers. If the latter look at worship as something magic that would take care of all human ills and aches instantaneously, they are absolutely right. But such an understanding is not Christianity's position. For the Eucharist offers a real source of spiritual, supernatural energy only to those who partake of it as an act of faith and love, first, to form a real union with Christ and among themselves, then, to step out of themselves and to carry the same energy outside the physical confines of the church and the territorial limits of the parish.[199]

Man left to his own natural resources is limited both in vision and accomplishments. If, however, a higher and deeper source of inspiration is made available to him, he can overcome his own limitations and reach out for people who otherwise would remain total strangers to him. And this is what worship and particularly the Eucharist is destined to make possible for him.

> It is by its worship that the Church lives, it is there that its heart beats. And in fact the life of the Church pulsates like the heart by systole and diastole. As the heart is for the animal body, so the cult is for church life a pump which sends into circulation and draws in again, it claims and it sanctifies. It is from the life of worship—from the Mass—that the Church spreads itself abroad into the world to mingle with it like leaven in the dough, to give it savor like salt, to irradiate like light, and it is towards the cult—towards the Eucharist—that the Church returns from the world, like a fisherman gathering up his nets or a farmer harvesting his grain. The only parochial activities which have any real justification are those which spring from worship and in their turn nourish it.[200]

Can we have a better image of the Eucharist than this pulsating heart of the celebrating Christian community?

Faith and love, the circulating blood that keeps the Christian alive and going, originates therein and returns to it for new pumping, for new mission. And in between pumpings it carries Christ's spirit on highways and byways to dispense Him as the source of energy and to draw all men to Him, the cause and sign of unity. Yes, the Eucharistic communion is the most fitting model of the parish-community for it symbolizes the here-and-now implementation of God's saving presence for mankind.

3) The Parish Is a Local Organization of the Universal Church

Approach to the Parish Based on Liturgy and Human Condition

The title of this model should not mislead the reader and create the impression that whatever we have said in this study so far will be contradicted or even negated on the following pages. Not at all. Though it is true that the above title could be read in a purely legalistic and minimalistic sense conceiving of the parish merely as the smallest organizational-administrative unit of the universal Church, it is not used here in this sense. Such a negative model of the parish could perhaps be claimed by inflexible canon lawyers, but certainly not by theologians.

It must be clear to the reader by now that the Church is understood here as a divine-human, historico-eschatological, and uniform-pluralistic reality which gives way to the natural and self-evident inference that, as the community of the Word-of-God-model leads to the community of the Eucharist-model, the two together must lead to their complementary counterparts, the models rooted in the human condition of man. These latter are simply necessary steps—not superior models—in the development and understanding of the parish as the conscious local self-actualization of the universal Church. As such, they can never replace the first two primary models of the parish dictated by the divine-revelatory constitutive element of the Church. But they can contribute greatly to their proper functioning and effective application by molding, conditioning, organizing, and making available the human element as the proper vehicle of the divine in the forming of the parish community.

We are making this statement fully aware of its conse- quences and also of the possible objections to its claim. Some people might take a position totally opposite to ours concerning the birth and development of the parish. Just to mention one example, we refer the reader to Daniel Calla- han who categorically denies, for instance, the primary role of the liturgy in the formation of the parish community; he also asserts that "it is the quality of the Christian life that the people and priests share" that actually leads to such community, "and this quality will be the direct result of their relations as human beings. How much do they love each other, rejoice with each other, share each other's bur- dens? That is the crucial question."[201]

Beautiful as this statement may be, it is very ambiguous and even misleading. If one reads it with a negative disposi- tion, it seems to stress only one half of the parish reality, i.e., the human condition that, as a starter, binds people together. But on this merely human level there is no specific need of the framework of the parish for fulfillment. If, however, one reads it with a positive disposition, the ex- pression "the quality of Christian life" already indicates an initial formation of those involved through their listening to the Word and their partaking of the Eucharist. In this interpretation, we fully support Callahan's position as veri- fying rather than negating our own thesis concerning the full integration of the divine and the human in the parish- experience.

Winter seems to take a stand similar to Callahan's when stating that

contrary to what some liturgists used to say, the celebration of the Eucharist does not create a community, it almost presupposes one. Or to put it more exactly, the two processes of celebrating Mass and building up a community are complementary.[202]

Again, we are puzzled by the same ambiguity and lack of clarity here as in the statement above. Winter seems to have overstretched his argument. For his reference to the presupposed community on which the parish can be built is only a good indication that the diaspora-situation is so much with us that we cannot expect to find homogeneous territorial communities any more. Parishes, therefore, should be created wherever natural or primary communities are available. But to stretch this situational fact into an argument and deny that the celebration of the Eucharist can and does become a community-building factor in the lives of the celebrating people is simply beyond comprehension. His statement also directly contradicts the conviction of the Council fathers that the parish

brings together the many human differences found within its boundaries and draws them into the universality of the Church. The laity should accustom themselves to working in the parish in close union with their priests, bringing to the church community their own and the world's problems as well as questions concerning human salvation, all of which should be examined and resolved by common deliberation.[203]

One can see at once that concerning the community aspect of the parish there exist two extremist approaches. Proponents of the first "argue that the supernatural, dynamic, and divine origin of the Church leave it essentially without comparison among human institutions," and as such it does not have to follow the patterns of other human organizations. Advocates of the second assert "that the problem with the Church is that it has not adopted enough of the modern organizational practices of other institutions,"[204] and therefore it can no longer cope with the behavior of modern man and contemporary society.

The former concentrate almost exclusively on the liturgy, the second on the natural or primary communities. Separated from each other they cannot operate successfully; working together harmoniously, they can become powerful and indestructible. Being aware of this, the Council strongly recommends that councils be established as far as possible on the parochial, interparochial, diocesan, and interdiocesan level as well as in the national or international sphere.[205]

In the fervor of renewal and the hope for shared responsibility, parish councils sprang up everywhere all over the United States after Vatican II. Some of them are still in operation, but many simply disappeared. The cause of their sudden demise was simple: one cannot start anything with structure if there is hardly anything there to be structured. Natural or primary groups are only the necessary first step, not the end-product. They too have to coalesce into the larger parish community with the help of the parish structure. But only those who *listen* to the Word and *celebrate* the Eucharist can really know the value and the need of human structure in the service of the community. Only they are really aware of the fact that the Kingdom needs them as its signs for its progressive and fuller realization.

In James O'Gara's words, they are "the thin edge of God's wedge"[206] that inserts God's Kingdom into the cultural, social world of the man come of age. A double duty for organization is implied in this call to push continuously for the realization of the Kingdom of God: (a) the internal organization of the community as such, to promote communion, cooperation, love, and unity among its members, and (b) the organization of the community as the sign or vehicle of God's Word and presence to the world. Our model includes both these aspects.

Internal Organization of the Parish Community

The internal organization of the parish community is necessitated by the human condition of the parishioners. The references above to the so-called primary groups or natural subcommunities have already indicated that more is needed for the theology of the parish and its effectiveness than the mere clerical and lay presence within it. Caution is especially required in regard to the clerical element, for by feeding the Word of God and the Eucharist to the community, priests can easily gain an upper hand in the life of the parish and even try to maintain or to bring back a preconciliar clerical dominance and paternalism. Such an attitude would greatly endanger even the first two models, but it would be totally destructive for the present one.

Furthermore, wherever human beings live and/or work together, their mutual interdependence is regulated by structures which they superimpose on themselves as a community. The supernatural community of the Church in general, and the parish in particular, is no exception. Just as interpersonal relationships are an absolute must for the individual to become a human person, and they are regulated by structure, so a living organism like the parish cannot grow, cannot even stay alive, without being regulated and structured in harmony with its purpose, i.e., to be the here-and-now local actualization of Christ's sacramental presence in the world, an eminently communitarian objective. Consequently, a model on this level should be conceived of in such a way that it would make cooperation of all or of some in the parish a reality by promoting "a deeper awareness of their shared humanity and Christianity."[207]

The pre- and postconciliar Church had known many efforts and experiments on the parish level toward giving due recognition to this shared humanity. Terms like parish council, parish board, parish committee or parish assembly are indications of such efforts.[208] The name does not really matter. What matters is the clear recognition of certain elements that must be understood, voluntarily accepted, and wholeheartedly supported by both clergy and laity within the parish. We find the following such elements important.

1) No excuse is acceptable for not having an adequate organizational setup in the parish. The arguments against it indicate only that the parish is handicapped by one of two misfortunes or perhaps even by both. The first is a deep-seated fear or at least uneasiness on the part of the priests who are unwilling to share their power or have no idea how to cope with lay presence in governing the parish. They trust nobody except themselves in spite of the fact that their performance hardly deserves recognition. The second is a hasty approach to the problem, an instantaneous creation of a parish council without necessary preparation of those who are suddenly called upon to participate actively and creatively in the life of the parish. Prestige, social recognition, self-seeking, and hunger for power rather than sharing the spirit of Christ and serving the community could influence the policies and decisions of such a group of people and sow the seeds of discord and power-struggle from the very beginning.

2) The organizational setup of the parish, grown out of the communion created by the Word of God and the Eucharist, is intended, in the first instance, to be a forum for dialogue; consequently, it should operate by consensus rather than by a mere plurality or majority of votes. Earlier in this chapter we have quoted the Decree on the Apostolate of the Laity which speaks of the parish as the instrument of *bringing together* the many differences preexisting within the parish. Bringing together does not result from counting votes but from dialoguing, in the process of which convictions and opinions are respected and a consensus is sought by all means.

3) In order to make the first two requirements come

true, members of the parish council must be committed to the Word of God and to the Eucharist. They are expected to be true believers and, on the level of their own cultural milieu, to be able to articulate their faith. Furthermore, it is essential that they be completely familiar with the updating of the Church and with important contemporary developments. For, in the words of the Council, "ceremonies however beautiful, or associations however flourishing, will be of little value if they are not directed toward educating men in the attainment of Christian maturity."[209]

The attainment of Christian maturity on the part of the members of the council will be reflected by their basic conviction of the necessity of the divine-human, historico-eschatological, clerical-lay elements working together harmoniously to enable the parish to function properly and effectively. Just as the local community would lose its very nature and purpose by refusing revelation as an essential part of its entire being, so it would become a mere remnant of the past without relevance for today by turning its back on the demands of a shared humanity.

4) As representatives of their coparishioners, members of the parish council have to consider themselves spokesmen of the community, speaking in their name and expressing their convictions, ideas, and visions. Yet they are expected to be leaders, hence men of conviction, decisiveness, and independence without ever mouthing the pastor's wishes or making him "into a mere errand boy for the parish" or always producing "the perfect solution for every problem."[210] Unfortunately,

> many Catholics, both laymen and priests, find it difficult to see how these contrasting emphases can work together in practice and both remain genuine. They point to many instances in which authoritarian and self-centered people, both priest and layman, manage to work within a facade of mutuality with others without really giving up their managing style, and

to other instances in which deeply rooted attitudes of submissiveness in parishes have, in spite of new structures, led to a situation in which everything important is still left to the pastor to decide.[211]

5) The greatest change that must take place within the parish is, therefore, a question of belief. Both priest and laity are called to the realization of the presence and workings of the Holy Spirit as *the* pulsating agent of the community. Since He speaks to the pastor through the laity and to the laity through the pastor, He does not speak two different languages. The Acts of the Apostles is a powerful witness of this basic truth of Christianity. A careful reading of chapters 2, 6, and 15 is particularly revelatory and inspiring in this regard.

All those present in the Upper Room received the Holy Spirit. All of them enjoyed the gift of speech. And all of them preached about the marvels of God. When problems emerged in the community of Jerusalem and the people turned to the apostles, the latter called a *full meeting* of the disciples and entrusted them with the privilege and duty of choosing seven reputable men for the service of the community. The fact that they refused to solve the problem without consultation is an excellent affirmation of their belief in the presence of the Spirit in the community and of their duty to listen to Him in their brethren.

The Council of Jerusalem is also an eminent example of how to allow the Spirit to manifest Himself in the operations of the community. When the controversy concerning circumcision and the dietetic laws developed at Antioch between the Christians of Hebrew origin and those of Gentile background, Paul and Barnabas were sent down to Jerusalem to seek an equitable solution. First, they were received "by the church," meaning evidently the whole community of believers, otherwise the apostles and elders would not have been mentioned separately by Luke. Then, the apostles *and* the elders together discussed the problems carefully, evidently in the presence of the whole assembly. Finally, when time came for a decision, it was James, the "brother of the Lord," and not Peter or one of the apostles who announced it to the assembly.

Most important of all, however, is the fact that in the message to the brothers of pagan origin at Antioch the participants in this first council used a phrase that should become the motto of every Christian community and particularly of every parish council: "It has been decided by the Holy Spirit and ourselves..." (Ac 15:28). They dared to say this because they had listened to one another's arguments during the long deliberation and the decision was no superimposition on anyone but a consensus reached by a community under the guidance of the Spirit manifesting itself in the nature of the arguments rather than in the mere counting of votes.

A parish structure is effective and a blessing to the community it is called to serve whenever its representatives can repeat with the Jerusalem community: "It has been decided by the Holy Spirit and ourselves...." Bearing this in mind, we can now understand the Council fathers' careful advice addressed especially to priests:

> Pastors also know that they themselves were not meant by Christ to shoulder alone the entire saving mission of the Church toward the world. On the contrary, they understand that it is their noble duty so to shepherd the faithful and recognize their services and charismatic gifts that all according to their proper roles may cooperate in this common undertaking with one heart.[212]

6) The common knowledge that the majority of the parishioners usually stay away from involvement in the deliberations and the works of the parish cannot be used to decline to form a parish council. Perhaps full cooperation was possible and even customary in previous homogeneous societies, but it is certainly not the rule of thumb of ours.

No organization in our culture can count on the active participation of the majority of its members, much less all of them. What is required is that the organization have enough of its members involved so that the job it has set for itself may be accomplished. From this point of view the goal of the parish is not to involve everyone, but rather to involve enough so that the parish's task may, at least in some fashion, be efficiently accomplished.[213]

In a diaspora-situation one can hardly hope for a majority participation. Nevertheless, the Holy Spirit can work effectively even with a minority, and use the involved people as leaven for the entire dough of the parish.

7) Finally, the point must be stressed that no parish organization, no parish council, should ever become exclusively parish-oriented. Superparochial, intra-parochial, diocesan, universal, civic, national, and human interests should also be its constant concern. The parish never ceases to be the bearer of the universal Church that is concretely actualized in its sacramental Eucharistic operations. Simultaneously, it is also the bearer of humanity for in its members humanity gains expression as it is experienced here and now, in a very particular situation, at a well-determined moment of history, with special cultural blessings or handicaps. And as long as these two elements are significant in the makeup of the parish, its leadership cannot forget interests transcending the confines of the parish. Many of those interests and problems cannot even be dealt with on the parish level. Yet they cannot be ignored for that reason, either.

Problems of the mass media, economic and social relations, racial justice, international peace, the underdeveloped countries—none of these are within the scope or the competence of the parish. The Church needs and needs rather desperately a vast assortment of techniques to meet the challenges of the twentieth century, and the parish is simply not suited for many

of these techniques. The parish can no longer be relied upon as the only or even the major level at which
the Church is engaged. The pious legend that the
parish priest is the only priest really on the front lines
should be forever put to rest.

It would seem to the present writer that our efforts
should be devoted not so much to making the parish
more like some ideal concept of what a community
should be, much less to lamenting the demise of community, but rather to taking whatever primary group
structure we have and opening it up to the needs of
the Church. It is not a question of building community so we may worship, nor of worshiping so that we
may have community, but rather of taking whatever
community we have and teaching it how to worship
and the meaning of worship so that it may go forth to
meet the problems of the larger community. Our
challenge, with some exceptions, is not to provide
more primary group experience, but to turn the primary group structure we have to the service of the Body
of Christ.[214]

The Parish as the Sign of God's Presence to the World

The fathers of Vatican II were anxious to recognize the
Catholic layman as having a twofold apostolate, one whose
two aspects are equally important and intrinsically related
to each other, i.e., "in the Church and in the world."[215] This
is not a privilege accorded to the laity by the hierarchy.
It is a right and duty derived from their incorporation into
the Mystical Body of Christ in the sacrament of Baptism
and from being strengthened by the Holy Spirit as Christians in the sacrament of Confirmation. The source and
authority of the commissioning is, therefore, the Lord Himself.[216]

The nature of the commissioning is large, even immense,
and cannot be considered as exclusively Church or parish
oriented. "Indeed, if the needs of cities and rural areas are

to be met, laymen should not limit their cooperation to the parochial or diocesan boundaries but strive to extend it to interparochial, interdiocesan, national, and international fields, the more so because the daily increase in population mobility, the growth of mutual bonds, and the ease of communication no longer allow any sector of society to remain closed in upon itself. Thus they should be concerned about the needs of the People of God dispersed throughout the world."[217]

In this regard, the same document expressly calls the parish "a kind of cell" of the diocese.[218] All the projects, activities, hopes, and dreams of the diocese depend on the parish for inspired workers, sustained effort, and relentless cooperation. As a matter of fact, the document, in reference to the national and international dimensions of the apostolate, calls the laity "the stewards of Christian wisdom," who should anxiously strive to promote the true common good, be loyal to their country, and faithfully fulfill their civic obligations. Public opinion should be their concern as well as participation in public affairs whenever they are qualified and called upon to do so.

Then, very significantly, the Council adds, "Catholics should try to cooperate with all men and women of good will to promote whatever is true and just, whatever is holy and worth loving (cf. Philippians 4:8). They should hold discussions with them, excelling them in prudence and courtesy, and initiate research on social and public practices which can be improved in the spirit of the gospel."[219] Finally, in order to promote "common human values," the laity are encouraged to cooperate not only with other Christians, but even with "men who do not profess Christ's name but acknowledge these values."[220]

Obviously, then, each parish, *in order to be* fully and truly Catholic, must now fulfill its own key role in this universal mission. This role of the Catholic parish is universal in two senses: (1) including all man's concerns, values and needs; (2) extending to all men, near and far, of all nations, cultures and convictions.[221]

The parish, as the here-and-now actualization of the universal Church and the sign of Christ's saving presence and power in the world, cannot cut itself off from its environment and turn in on itself. It is standing in between the Church and the world having one foot in each of those two larger realities, and offering something to both, i.e., revelation, the historical dimension, to mankind, and to the Church the actual needs to which the Church has to speak. Consequently, the parish, in addition to its internal structure, must have the interest in and the predisposition for larger external relational structures. This basic requirement covers many problems and suggests basic reorientations on the level of the parish—even for the sake of the parishioners in whose life the human condition plays an important and predominant role.

Writing about the "in-migration" and "out-migration" of Catholic families in suburbia, and describing their uprooted state of mind, Marvin Bordelon remarks pointedly that

> the Catholic begins to wonder about the *relevance* of his Church to his own personal situation. What does the Church have to say to the modern world? To him? How does the Church serve him? How does the Church serve him, as he is, now? . . . . The real Christ becomes increasingly obscured in the trappings of organized religion, of religion seemingly organized for the sake of the Establishment.[222]

What, then, is the first requirement for the parish to open itself up to structures other than its own internal setup? The initial step should be the intense study of the environment, of the area in which the parish is located, with its religious, cultural, historical, social, political, economic, racial, and national background. For the parish cannot be reduced to those who participate in the liturgical celebrations on Sunday. "It is an *area* first of all, for the people cannot be abstracted from the area in which they live. To get a true picture of the parish one must observe the rhythm of life that goes on within the area of the parish."[223] That rhythm speaks not only of everyday problems enveloping the lives of the laity but also of their outlook on life, their expectations, their own understanding of themselves, in brief, the prevailing conscience of mankind at the present stage of historical development.

The second requirement is a complete change in our understanding in regard to the missionary nature of the Church. The community as such is the bearer of that mission. And the community's greatest part is the laity. The inference is evident: either they carry Christ's spirit into the world or the missionary spirit is practically dead. Michael Winter, ruminating on unfortunate historical developments in the Church in this regard, remarks: "It is instructive to ask ourselves when it was that the lay person ceased to be the normal missionary for Christianity. It was probably in the fourth century that he last exercised this role satisfactorily."[224] As a consequence of it, the whole educational system of the Church has become self-centered and truncated in its scope and purpose, particularly wherever the Catholic Church finds itself in a minority-status as in almost all English-speaking countries: the educational contribution of Catholic teachers, especially members of religious orders, is confined within the Catholic schools.

They have thereby cut themselves off from the milieu in which they could exercise both witness to the gospel and apostolate. In a country like England this is very serious. The number of committed Christians of all churches is small in comparison with the population of the whole nation, which means that the task of educating children is being to some extent left to those who have less spiritual idealism. This is happening at a time when society as a whole is becoming more and more godless and when young people are exposed to temptations which are appalling. It is strange that nobody has seen how much this is at variance with the message of the gospels. Christ told his followers that they must go out into the highways and byways of the city, and that they must act as the leaven in the whole loaf. Nowhere does the gospel tell Christians to create a secure ghetto. In countries which are entirely Catholic this problem does not become apparent, but when we are a minority group we must ask ourselves seriously, "By what right do we withdraw our presence from society as a whole?" In the field of education it means that we have in effect deprived the nation of the opportunity of sharing our spiritual treasures.[225]

The man of today is conditioned differently from the man of previous times. The means of communication and transportation make it possible for him to be ubiquitous. He travels and is informed instantaneously of other peoples' convictions and of happenings all over the world. As a result, he has become a man of global conscience. He enters other men's lives and others enter his. This man can enjoy parish life only if there, too, the global aspect of human orientation gains expression and is responded to constructively. Consequently, solidarity of Catholics and Christians must be complemented with solidarity of all men even on the parish level. This is possible only if and when the parish embraces both internal and external structures and favors complete and mutual interaction between the universal Church and the world of man.

4) The Parish Is a Community Restructured into Small Subcommunities

Created by Structural Changes in Parish and Diocese

In developing the model of the parish as the community gathered together to celebrate the Eucharist, we mentioned the necessity of finding primary groups or natural subcommunities within the parish and utilizing them as important subcenters to further the Eucharistic orientation and formation of the entire parish community. In this approach the stress was on the *natural* characteristic of these groups. They are there on their own and they have to be discovered. Discussion clubs, marriage encounter people, student groups, teenagers, nursing homes, hospitals, professional people, etc. can be considered natural groups within the larger local entity. The subcommunity idea offers, however, another possible approach to the problem of the parish, i.e., their creation from above, and in this way, too, they bear the possibilities of a different model.

No effort toward the renewal of the parish can be expected to succeed unless it meets with the cooperation, goodwill, and wholehearted support of the higher authorities in the Church. This means that, while the parish priests and the people try their very best to study their area and apply the first three models accordingly, Church authorities must do their utmost to create a favorable atmosphere for the models by promoting structural changes both on the parochial and on the diocesan level. Is such a dream possible today? We intend to explore such possibilities by giving serious consideration to the nature of the problem.

The Approach of Michael Winter

Michael M. Winter's *Blueprint for a Working Church—A Study in New Pastoral Structures* appeared on the American market in 1973[226] with the claim of offering principles for restructuring parish life which are applicable "to all churches working in de-Christianized nations." It is hardly a disputed question any more that the United States is one of those countries. Winter's ideas should, therefore, be of special interest to Americans.

One of the signs of the de-Christianized status quo is the frequent use of the term "post-Christian" in contemporary literature. It seems to indicate a very perplexing situation for the observer. "Too often it is assumed that the nation is basically Christian by habit, or alternatively that it is pagan. Neither of these assessments is correct. The evangelization of religious-minded pagans in a continent like Africa is totally different from the task of giving basic religious values to a culture which was formed by Christianity in the past, but whose people have for the most part rejected its tenets."[227] What is the cause of this perplexing situation? The very fact that "the standard patterns of parish, diocese, and religious order, which we now use, were fixed in the medieval period."[228] Hence, the structures have to be refashioned in line with contemporary awareness and requirements.

Stressing the structure-element out of proportion can lead to dangerous misunderstanding, and Winter is conscious of it. No, mere structural reshaping of the Church would not solve the many problems the believing Christian faces today. "Structures are not the answer to all problems. Personal attitudes are just as important. Conversion occurs, after all, in the person, not in the organization."[229] But personal interest and conversion must be supported by suitable structures. If these are absent, even the most fervent persons might find themselves out of place in an unsupportive parish. Winter, then, proposes the following fourfold program as a theological rule of thumb of the Church: the Church, and consequently the parish, "must be a community of worship, charity, witness, and apostolate."[230]

Actually, with the help of a little imagination, these could be paralleled with our first four models though they can hardly be called models themselves. They are rather criteria with the help of which models can be tested and verified. Even Winter admits that they "do not tell us immediately what sort of community is needed. They are merely a method of breaking down the fundamental Christian vision into manageable concepts which can be easily grasped."[231]

This theological rule of thumb is pregnant with implications. For if the immediate objectives of satisfactory worship, charity, witness, and apostolate are recognized as indispensable criteria of community life, and if the ideas of renewal and theological direction of Vatican II are taken seriously, certain conclusions for the parish are inevitable. What are these conclusions?

1) "The basic community must be small, consisting of about twenty or thirty people."[232] Anything larger than that would hinder creating close-knit communities. This first conclusion only reinforces Winter's conviction, mentioned above, that personal or moral renewal is impossible without renewal of structure. He believes so strongly in this assumption that he further contends that the renewal intended by Vatican II must be carried out primarily "in the realm of structures." Presently, neither the parish nor the diocese is geared to creating communities; therefore, they must be altered structurally. Today's parish, for example, is obviously "of an unworkable size": too large for satisfactory Eucharistic celebrations and too small for other purposes, such as education or youth work.[233] Winter particularly stresses the point that it is witnessing and the apostolate that have suffered most from the limitations built into the present parish system:

> It seems an inescapable fact that parishes were only set up after the nations of Europe had been converted and when the missionary period was at an end. This may well mean that an authentic mission (to convert non-believers) will not start again until the parish structure has been superseded by something more dynamic.[234]

2) In reference to Eucharistic celebrations, he claims that normally they should take place in private houses with no more than twenty or thirty people present. In addition to this *normal* celebration, the people involved should meet occasionally in larger groups "to fortify the sense of the Church's unity." Then, at regular intervals, all the Catholics in the same town should share one Eucharist. The reader should notice at once the term "the same town." Instead of

"the same parish" Winter uses the term "the same town" indicating that he expects substantial changes in the parish structure. Finally, at less frequent intervals, the whole diocese should celebrate Mass with the bishop. The reason for this is very simple. "If a diocese is not in some sense a Eucharistic community, then an important element is absent from its theological constitution."[235]

3) How are we to translate the above liturgical considerations into territorial concreteness? Winter deals with this question on three levels: in towns, in cities, and in rural areas. For him, these are the "natural social groupings" that ecclesiastical divisions of territory should follow in principle.

Serving the people of cities effectively requires that a medium-size town of seventy or eighty thousand inhabitants form only one pastoral unit. It should be divided into six to ten pastoral subunits, each of them entrusted to one particular priest. The priests, however, would live together and work as a team. These subunits are the area within which the basic cells of twenty or thirty people could be grouped.

Cities with a quarter of a million or more inhabitants should be dioceses in their own right, and carefully divided into pastoral units, subunits, and basic cells, following the pattern established above. The same procedure should be followed in what he calls "monster cities of the dimensions of London or New York" with the noteworthy exception that they should be broken up first into several dioceses. Here is his text in reference to towns and cities:

> The easiest case to consider is the medium-sized town of seventy or eighty thousand inhabitants. Towns of this size should not be subdivided into independent parishes, but the whole area should be treated as one pastoral unit. The clergy should live together and work as a team. . . . Within this pastoral unit further divisions should be made, six or ten of them perhaps,

which would be much smaller than the present parishes with which we are familiar.

Each division would be entrusted to one priest with whom the people could identify, thus avoiding the imprecise situation of many large parishes at present, where a district may be vaguely under the care of four or five priests, not one of whom is clearly responsible for a specific part. These divisions within the town are not yet the basic community, but they would provide the area within which the basic cells of twenty or thirty people could be grouped. With this three-tier structure for the average-sized town, all the activities of the Church's mission could be discharged properly.

At the other end of the scale, cities whose population is a quarter of a million or more should be dioceses in their own right. Within their boundaries pastoral units (like the medium-sized town) would have to be established, after very careful attention had been given to the delineating of boundaries. Monster cities of the dimensions of London or New York would require yet another grouping, whereby several dioceses could be coordinated into a larger working unit. This has already been done in Paris, and it is a system which merits application elsewhere.[236]

Rural areas are not so simple to deal with; therefore, the one-priest parishes should be continued there. Villages, however, should be treated as "intermediate zones in the towns," i.e., as having pastoral subunits and within the subunits basic cells. In this way, the natural sense of unity of a village could be respected.[237]

4) Restructuring the parish and the diocese greatly depends on the availability of priests. Basic cells cannot operate without them. But presently the shortage of priests is an ever-deepening problem of the Church, and can jeopardize any possible planning for the future unless something is done about it.

The atmosphere in which the Church must operate today is the post-Christian or diaspora situation which calls for a missionary spirit and for priests who can be shaped by this present situation rather than being shaped by medieval ideas and ideals far removed from the condition of modern man.

In this regard two possibilities are open to the Church. The first one would be a simple redistribution of priests according to the demands of restructuring the parish and the diocese as explained in (3) above. The second would tap a new source of vocations, i.e., men who have already proven their worth by emerging as the natural leaders of their basic cells would be ordained to the priesthood. In most cases these would be married men, blessed with natural ability, dedication, and a great sense of communication. They would continue to earn their living in their profession, and, on a part-time basis, they would also function as ministers of the basic cells. If such a recommendation is ever accepted and tried in the Church, full-time priests would be needed only as clerical leaders of pastoral subunits or coordinators of all the basic units found in one pastoral area.

5) Finally, Winter approaches, "with some trepidation," the problem of the diocese and claims that one bishop to about fifty priests should be the upper limit. His leading reason falls in line with our thinking because it incorporates the first two models, particularly the second one, which we have worked out earlier on these pages. Winter's position is that "if the diocese is to possess a sense of unity, it must be in some way a Eucharistic community."[238] He refers to Ignatius of Antioch's theological position according to which the bishop's role in the unity of the Church is most prominent in his Eucharistic role. The consequence is that the people of the diocese must be able to celebrate the Eucharist together at least occasionally, "bringing together the majority of the population." In the present structural setup of the dioceses such an event is hardly possible; there-

fore, the diocese "cannot be regarded as a Eucharistic community in any meaningful sense. If the Eucharist is not the high point of its unity, it is difficult to conceive of any other basis for it which would satisfy the patristic tradition."[239]

Winter, then, sums up his position as follows:

> As in antiquity, the bishop would live at the principal church in the main city of his region, thus ensuring that he was personally immersed in the apostolate to the people. The concept of the 'diocesan office' must vanish, and these small dioceses would make use of the curial office of the metropolitan. The fifty or so priests with whom the bishop worked would be grouped in perhaps six or ten teams, providing one team for each medium-sized town, possibly two or three for a city, and smaller groups, or one-man parishes, for rural areas.[240]

Obviously, such a position, if executed, would have great repercussions for the makeup of the entire Church. Small dioceses, for one, should be grouped together to find mutual support and to share curial offices and similar services. Such a development could bring back, in some form or other, the distinction and the line of power of country bishops, ordinary bishops of the cities, metropolitans, and patriarchs, readjusted of course to contemporary conditions and expectations. It would be necessary furthermore, that intermediary groupings be created between the national episcopal conferences and the dioceses to make the work of such conferences possible and effective. Finally, a new concept and approach should be developed for calling ecumenical councils because the extremely high number of bishops would make their numerical presence practically impossible. Yet, Winter asserts, "the requirements of this institution must yield to the demands of a satisfactorily organized territorial episcopate, since the former is not of divine origin, whereas the bishops' ordinary authority is derived from Christ."[241]

Critical Evaluation of Winter's Approach

We take it for granted that the reader has already raised in his or her mind many objections to the viability of Winter's understanding of the parish and the diocese and of his recommendations for restructuring both. The objections could concern, first of all, the parish itself. Is he realistic enough by restricting the so-called basic cells to twenty or thirty people? And more importantly, is it possible to envision these basic cells merely on the ground of location? The very fact that people happen to live together physically in the same building or on the same block could be advantageous to the creation of basic cells among them. But the contrary also could be true. When animosity develops between neighbors, it is hard to imagine that they would be looking forward to an intimate celebration together unless, naturally, they are perfect Christians who profoundly believe in the healing power of the Eucharist and are anxious to apply it to their own particular situation.

An objection could also be raised in regard to the minister of these basic cells. It seems even to this writer that, practically speaking, pastoral work in its entirety would be carried out by the part-time ministers of the cells. Actually, they would be in direct contact with the people. The priests in charge of the pastoral subunits would meet the people only occasionally. It is possible, therefore, that the notion of the office-type priest that Winter is so anxious to eliminate would be preserved in another form.

Doubt could also be expressed in reference to Winter's high hopes as far as the number of part-time priests is concerned. Though several basic cells could be taken care of by the same minister, for example, several city blocks or a cluster of apartment buildings, the high number of the cells would require a relatively high number of priests. It is at least doubtful that ordaining trusted married men to the priesthood would solve the problem.

But the life-style of the priests in charge of the pastoral subunits is also questionable. In Winter's understanding, they would live together as a community, apart from their own pastoral subunits. The reader might be right in taking a negative stand on such a proposition. After all, not even full-time priests committed themselves to the community life-style of religious. Furthermore, their pastoral work could suffer from such an arrangement. If their availability is hindered in any way, either by distance or by community commitments, the hoped-for-results of the restructuring of the parish could hardly materialize.

The toughest part of the whole new outlook, however, is the reorganization of the diocese. No matter whether the reader questions the wisdom of fifty as the upper limit of the number of priests attached to it or the size of the diocese, objections could pop up everywhere; questions could even be raised in regard to vacating diocesan offices or to grouping small dioceses together for mutual support and for common offices. Would not these small dioceses simply replace powerful large parishes in the present system? Would the bishops of the small dioceses remain independent or would they be interfered with by the metropolitans who would reduce them to the status of country bishops of ancient times? These and other possible questions indicate only the rather serious problems underlying Winter's unusual approach to the restructuring of the parish and diocese.

One must be blind or at least insensitive to the issues of pastoral life emerging in the whole complex of parish life not to see the latent great value of Winter's effort. The details of what he says in his book may be ignored or seriously questioned by the reader; the model itself, however, must be recognized as highly realistic and rooted in the correct understanding of vital issues of human and Christian life on two grounds. It is a positive response, first, to the demands of the interlocking reality of the human condition and divine revelation and, second, to the pressures of the contemporary understanding of the mission of the Church.

The whole book is eminent testimony to Winter's taking the human condition very seriously. The chapter on the clergy (pp. 70-113) is particularly impressive and convincing. "If there is one lesson," he writes, "which is absolutely clear from the history of theology, it is the importance of a realistic contact with the culture of society in general. The Fathers owe their theological excellence in no small measure to their pagan education. Their minds were not corrupted in these schools but broadened."[242]

On this basis, Winter advances his conviction that the medieval structures of the parish and of the Church in general have had a paralyzing effect even on the contemporary Church because they have been preserved while the conditions that had created them are long gone and forgotten. If it is true that structures are created by concrete needs and situations, i.e., by cultural, sociological, political, and economic factors that evoke a certain kind of consciousness on the part of men affected by those factors, it is also crystal-clear that structures must be changed and updated with the changing consciousness and the altered nature of the contributing factors.

Only with the help of such updated structures can the contemporary man be expected to respond positively and creatively to his own needs and situations. Now, it goes without saying that today's society can hardly be compared with the society of the Middle Ages. The consciousness of today's man is far different from what is known to us as the consciousness of the man of the Middle Ages. How, then, can the Church react and respond to such a new reality? Is it enough merely to call for a moral renewal? Not at all, says Winter. Moral renewal does not and cannot come unless structural changes take place first to enable the contemporary Christian to develop as both fully human and fully Christian.

Obviously, the primary place for such changes is the parish itself where the Church meets the real man, the existential man in his concrete, everyday situation, and where the same man is called upon to respond to his calling with the fourfold criteria of the Church's effective presence in any given situation of any age, time, or culture, i.e., with worship, charity, witness, and apostolate. While God's self-revelation in Jesus Christ remains the same in its historicity today and tomorrow, the interpretation, personal and social meaning, applicability, and translation of that revelation requires its mutual complementarity with the human condition. This Winter has understood clearly as perhaps the most basic problem of contemporary Christianity and tried to approach the question of structure in view of it.

This brings us to the second positive factor in Winter's analysis of the parish, namely, his correct understanding of the mission of the Church *today* as it is dictated by both its revelational and human element.

If we take seriously terms like "anonymous Christian," "post-Christian world," "minority Christianity," or "diaspora-situation" and reflect on their meaning, we find that only primitive Christianity experienced something similar to our world and the Church's situation therein. Practically speaking, the Church faces today, too, a pagan world around it. Though we still like to call certain countries Christian, such a characterization refers more to the past of these countries than to their present, for society in any country has ceased to be guided by traditionally Christian principles. And the terms used above specifically refer to this new phase in the history of the Church and the parish.

Consequently, the most urgent question today is what to do about and how to respond to the diaspora or post-Christian situation of the Church. If a choice is forced upon us between effective mission and traditional structure, which one are we to choose? Winter never doubts for a second that mission should always prevail over traditional structure. The whole history of the Church, at least the constructive periods of that history, testify to it.

Such a position reflects the conviction that the structural elements of the Church, over and above the minimal interpretation of some presence of visible structure as the incarnation of the supernatural, are always in a process of developing. This process should never be stilled or aborted, for such a forcible intervention would greatly hinder the full realization of the very mission of the Church. Unfortunately, experience shows that "the revolutionary upsurge of urban technical life has outpaced the Christian response"[243] to an incredible degree. We have stood by watching society change rapidly and even radically without really trying to change our ecclesiastical structures accordingly. No wonder, then, that we have been left behind, almost hopelessly behind.

Winter, together with many others, has realized the disastrous outcome of our passive waiting and has reached back into the history and theology of the primitive Church for ideas and inspiration. Then he has reached out to his contemporaries, to us, offering his understanding of the solution of the problem. He has done so "with trepidation," knowing full well that the model emerging from his thoughts will be resented and rejected by many. But resentment and rejection cannot invalidate the model itself. And this writer hopes that at least some of the ideas and thoughts presented here will generate further inquiries into the grave question of how to promote moral renewal by reaching out for basic structural changes first.

5) The American Parish: the Agent of Change

This study would not be complete without an inquiry into the nature and function of the American parish. The fifth and last model will, therefore, be devoted entirely to this important and vital topic.

Casiano Floristan, following Le Bras' elements of religious sociology,[244] formulates four main factors that intervene in man's life, even in its most personal and religious dimension. They are the social, psychological, geographical, and historical realities of the human world, i.e., society, psyche, space, and time, as influencing and transforming factors of both individual and communal life. In their community-affecting dimension, the same elements are also

active and determining factors in the formation and operation of a parish.[245]

Apart from the apostolic Church, it would be very hard
to find another period of Christian history better or more
favorably influenced by the above factors than the one which
began with the discovery and populating of the North American Continent, especially the United States of America.
Here the real possibility of a genuine and creative new start
was entirely present, unhindered by previously developed
regulations, and centuries-old customs and usages. In the
New World it became evident from the very beginning of
the Christian presence that the message of revelation and
the demands of the human condition had to work hand in
hand as mutually important co-agents of the divine presence
in order to respond forcefully and creatively to the hopes,
aspirations, trials, and tribulations of the people involved
in the new situation. Unfortunately, the opportunity was
not always recognized by those to whose care the infant
American church was entrusted either by divine providence
or by chance.

Historical Hindsight

No organized Catholic Church and no organized parishes
existed in the United States until after the Revolutionary
War. As a matter of fact, "early history does not record large
voluntary migrations of individual groups. Those who came
maintained their religious practices in their adopted country
to the best of their ability, or eventually lost their faith
entirely."[246] One can only guess at the number of those who
actually lost their faith; but considering the circumstances,
it must have been very high.

Two historical incidents in particular, among others,
contributed greatly to this loss. First, in the pre-Revolution-
ary War period there were, except in Maryland, relatively
few Catholics in the United States, and they were scattered
all over the entire territory. Second, priests were scarce,

had to cover large territories, and were obliged to work from mission-centers rather than fully established territorial parishes. In this early period the Catholic Church depended entirely on Europe for both financial help to found missions and for priests and religious to take care of those missions.

It is true that the situation changed greatly with the appointment of John Carroll as Prefect Apostolic in 1784 and as the first American bishop of the diocese of Baltimore in 1789. However, the problems that had tormented the missions and the quasi-parishes remained unabated even after the appointment. Dissension, factionalism, distrust, and quarrels protruded their ugly heads everywhere, but mostly in three specifically American problems created by the overflow of people to the new land of promise: trusteeism, rival nationalities, and the free-lance clerics.[247]

These problems have been dealt with in American and Church history.[248] For our study a general history of the parish in the United States is not of prime importance. Nonetheless, the early American atmosphere and situation in which the parish developed and the opportunity America offered to priests and bishops to create new structures demanded by and responding to the unparalleled situation found in the United States are crucially important.[249]

In view of Vatican II's debate on the nature of the Church, some of the theological convictions and theses expressed clearly and forcefully at this early stage of American history are striking. Since the laity usually preceded the clergy in moving into new regions, particularly on the American frontiers, they were conscious of their diaspora-situation and of their minority role in a hostile environment. Without resident priests to advise them, they were left to their own initiative and ingenuity. They lived in relative independence from the hierarchy, so to speak, and their newly gained political freedom and experience in the new republican nation colored and noticeably influenced their Christian conviction and their ecclesiastical outlook. All these unusual elements contributed, then, to an understanding of lay-responsibility for the Church.[250] This was something good, a return to the primitive Church's self-understanding. This positive trend should be readily recognized and accepted in spite of some unfortunate negative features that clouded up the entire issue of lay involvement in early American history.

Two factors should be mentioned here from the theological thought-pattern of one of the most controversial lay theologians this land has ever produced, Dr. John F. Oliveira Fernandez. First is his claim that the layman's role in the affairs of the Church derives from "experience and the nature of things." The overriding importance of this factual principle in his eyes led him to the further assertion that the layman, precisely because of his experience and the nature of things, was more qualified than Church officials to become an agent of transformation and reform within the Church.[251] Second, on this ground, he objected to the clerical domination of his day as anti-scriptural and alien to the practices of the primitive Church. What he perceived as most needed for reform and transformation was a return to original integrity and innocence by restoring the laity to their role and dignity in the Church as the union of the faithful.

Evidently, Fernandez saw change and development as essential features of the Church, particularly on the operational level of local community. Had his vision been accepted and institutionalized, the layman could have functioned as an essential link between Church and world by mediating effectively between the free democratic republic of the United States and the faithful followers of the Catholic Church. It is at least possible that such development would have facilitated the creation of a Pastoral Constitution on the Church in the Modern World with less agonizing and much earlier than Vatican II.

Unfortunately, the good and well-intentioned though unfounded and unjustified theological and structural claims advanced by Fernandez and his associates blinded the American hierarchy to his insightful perception of the role of the Catholic Church in the extraordinary situation of the New World. Only God knows what might have happened had his insights into the importance of the human condition and into Church and world relationship been grasped, corrected, and creatively applied. Instead, they were first ignored, then condemned in their entirety, and stamped for good as alien to Catholic thought and practice. Though Bishop John England tried his very best to respond creatively to the unusual situation of the Church in the United States, the final outcome of the entire issue was influenced more by Archbishop Ambrose Marechal of Baltimore and the majority of the hierarchy siding with him. Most of the hierarchy supported Marechal's authoritarian attitude toward issues rather than England's more positive attitude formulated in The Constitution of the Roman Catholic Church of North Carolina, South Carolina and Georgia.[252]

In this respect, the argument that the American bishops were so tightly controlled by the Congregation for the Propagation of the Faith that they were unable to make decisions advocated by the entirely new situation of the United States simply does not hold water. As a matter of fact,

> the bishop was the supreme head of the diocese and, though he could not legislate contrary to the general law, or without grave reason dispense from the general observance, he was in a position to judge the immediate conditions which made possible such observance, and could interpret the law in its conditions over which he was guardian.[253]

The greatness of Bishop England rests in the fact that he used his position to judge the actual conditions of Christian life and did not allow the negative and destructive elements to prevent him from grasping the possible good present in the demands. His Constitution unequalled and certainly unsurpassed to this day, has remained a lasting monument to his active understanding of and deep interest in the constructive cooperation of clergy and laity dictated by the human condition as it was experienced by Catholics in the New World.[254]

It is indeed a tribute to this outstanding prelate that he was perspicacious enough to have sensed the following: (1) The people needed written laws to be protected from authoritarian, arbitrary application of power. (2) Voluntaryism lay at the very heart of American participation in life as the concrete rendition of the outcome of a diaspora-situation. (3) The basic equality of clergy and laity had again surfaced as an undeniable feature of Christian and Catholic life. (4) Instead of mere status, competence and personal merit should be the ground of acceptance of and appreciation for the clergy by the laity. (5) The democratic process and framework of this country made it mandatory for both clergy and laity to participate in the decision-making processes in the Church. (6) Participation was not a favor granted by the hierarchy but a basic Christian right rooted in the fundamental equality of all Christians.

Therefore, while the extremist Trustee-concept stressed the layman's official capacity in the Church as manager of temporal affairs, as agent of reform, and as independent interpreter of the Church-world relationships, England's concept of the layman stressed the latter's participating partnership, valuable experience, and cooperation in temporal and spiritual upbuilding of the Church. Both of these concepts attributed tremendous importance to the respectful dealing with the human condition and to the changed and changing situation of the faithful requesting a similar attitude on the part of those who acted in the name of the Church.

How regretful it is that this built-in device of the American local community for promoting change in line with the times was ignored by the majority of the hierarchy at a time that was unique in the entire history of mankind! Instead, a third concept of the layman was promoted and enforced officially throughout the United States, that of the passive layman who was called upon to do only two things: to support his church financially and to submit himself passively to Church authorities without ever dreaming of participatory democracy coming to him in his parish.[255]

As one looks back at these fateful years of the early American parish life, it becomes clear that they represent a golden opportunity offered to and refused by the American Church. The reason for this refusal was simple. The Catholic Church did not have a theology of the parish, only regulations concerning its canonical entity. Consequently, Church officials did not know how to deal with a situation which demanded a theological and not just a juridical solution. There were not too many gifted individuals to be found who could sense and give expression to the extraordinary presenting itself under the guise of the ordinary.[256] While Fernandez was guilty of seeing and judging everything in the light of the new situation in spite of the fact that he was an ardent student of the Bible and history, the majority of the American hierarchy approached the same problem exclusively from the viewpoint of revelation.

It is pitiful to see that the layman might have recognized God's hand in the possibilities offered to him in the American situation more readily than the men of God especially trained to speak in His name and with His authority. As my eminent student, Dr. Patrick Carey, put it so eloquently:

> The layman ... [became] a revealer of new insights into the Christian message. The experience of the world of democratic and republican forms of government helped the layman to see his Christian life in a new perspective and forced him to read the scriptures and tradition with a new awareness of freedom and equality. In this way his human experience in a new world (the political world) became a source of revelation for him. He, therefore, sought to reform the Church in light of those experiences and in conformity with what he discovered in scripture and Church history. His initiatives, although not entirely

in conformity with Catholic tradition, revealed a dimension of God's will for his people that has only recently been widely accepted.[257]

All this clearly indicates that the profound desire for change and changing has been a pronounced feature of American parish life from the very beginning of its existence. Like the pioneering spirit, industrialization and technology, and in particular the systems of communication and transportation, have dominated the American scene and American life. The rapid changes wrought by them made themselves felt, if not positively, at least negatively, in the disappointing alienation of the intellectuals and the young, in the very midst of the parish. For whenever the American parish refused to function as the agent of change, dark and impenetrable clouds prevented the parishioners from seeing the meaning of their getting involved in the life of the local parish community.

The full realization of this basic fact is so important for the life of the local church-community that without formulating it correctly one cannot even hope to move ahead and offer intelligent alternatives to the parishioners. The old habit of looking at the Church merely as the agent *reflecting* on the Christ-event that happened once in the past several millenia simply has to go. The Church, especially its local realization and actualization in the form of the celebrating community, is the living embodiment of that Christ-event that must be experienced anew in order to grasp and communicate its significance to contemporary men and women. And if the psychologist's claim that "a generation now lasts about seven years" is justified, no sincere believer can be slow in drawing the obvious conclusion that

if God's self-disclosure in Jesus Christ is to make any sense at all to a constantly changing culture and society, then revelation must undergo a continual historical and critical examination, together with the twentieth century to which it is proclaimed.[258]

The temptation to minimize the impact and importance of change always remains real and strong. One likes to give preference to the known and possessed. The unknown and the unconquered look enticing only to the courageous and the visionary. But these are the people who are able to study the past with their eyes on the future, and to excavate unfailing treasures and erect them into new cathedrals of the future. With them in mind and in view of the past of the American Church, one can state flatly and firmly that

> we cannot rely upon the happy principle so often utilized in the past that given time, the course of human affairs will right itself. When there is disparity between change and institutional adjustment in the modern world, the peril of dissolution and disorder is immediate, for the whole pace of invention, change, and renovation does not wait upon the passage of time. Change itself is a principle of our society, and life must be lived in response to it.[259]

But how can one become the agent of change? How can the principle of change be envisioned as lying at the very heart of parish-life, transforming the local community into an agent of change? For this, one must look at what lies ahead for the parish and for the Church. Only then can one try to grapple with the vexing question: What must be done today, here and now, to bridge the gap between past indications and future expectations? A realistic look at the American parish of the future is, therefore, very much in order at this point of the study of the parish.

Future Expectations

Our look at the history of early America indicates very clearly that the human condition has played a remarkable role in the life of the Church in America. God has used the laity and the entirely new situation found nowhere else in modern history to reveal the workings and influence of His Spirit in guiding history itself and developing new trends in the Church. Though the response of the hierarchy to the new revelatory situation was rather timid, hesitant, even authoritarian and inimical more often than not, one still can state confidently and without exaggeration that in the United States

> the Church was able to reveal again something of her rich personality. By examining with clinical precision every human condition, she could uncover the deep affinity of correspondence existing between the authentic expression of 'human-ness' and the fullness of her own truth and life. She could bring a unity which transcended all human variety and differentiation, one which, being divine, could not destroy this human variety, but fulfilled it and made it intelligible and meaningful.[260]

The interaction between the supernatural operation of the Word and grace of God and the actuality of the human condition has been greatly experienced in the life of the local communities created on American soil. If any one thing has been learned from this experience it can be summed up in the conclusion that the Church cannot start its operations "from where she thinks people should be, but from where they actually are, i.e., in a form of society largely man-made and in a world ruled by its own natural laws. Society and the world in which men live were already in existence before the Church. They cannot be bypassed in the life of any parish of the Church. No parish can live its own self-enclosed life as though the society and the world in which it exists were of no consequence."[261]

What does this mean for the future of the American parish? William J. Sullivan, S.J., in an important address to the Joint Pastoral Conference of the Dioceses of Madison and La Crosse, Wisconsin, at Madison, June 15, 1971, faced this question and singled out three factors, already perceptibly present in our culture and potentially influential in the future.[262]

1) In contrast to the present preoccupation with the question of authority, "the shape of the Church tomorrow, of the Church of 2000, will be determined most profoundly by the nature of and direction of the metamorphosis of authority in the Catholic Church." Though several factors will contribute to such a process, it is important to note that "in the United States the most basic factor is a *cultural phenomenon,* a natural and necessary effect of the kind of world in which we live. Religion and culture are closely and thoroughly interrelated, and our culture is a democratic culture." It follows that such a democratic metamorphosis will be whole-heartedly welcome and embraced by members of the believing and worshiping communities.[263]

2) The second factor is "the implosion of personal religious freedom" meaning "the penetration, permeation of freedom into every aspect of the religious life of the Church." In reference to the mediating function of the Church as the sacrament of Christ, Sullivan makes two particularly incisive observations that might have incalculable relevance to the Christian of the future and his personal attitude toward his religious community. First, he notes, that "it is possible to concentrate on the notions of Transcendent God and Mediating Church to the point of losing sight of Man. One must not forget that man is *mediated* and also *mediating.*" Second, "the Catholic Christian knows and asserts that the religious act must be his. It is not enough that it be an act of 'the Church,' an act out there. It must be his hearing, his acceptance, his response if it is to be his prayer, his worship." For "the Church does not act for the individual in the sense of acting *in place of* the individual. She acts *for the sake of* the individual Christian, for his benefit. She is propaedeutic, not vicarious."[264]

Then, to stress further his point, he introduces the interesting distinction between the settlers and the searchers, reflecting the kind of culture that produces them. Because ours is an age of transition, change, and movement forward, the concept of finished man, promoted and supported by the spirit of Trent, is definitely over. "Now we are coming to sense the unfinished nature of Christian man, of our relation to God, of the body of Christ to which we belong. We are living in pain. The demand for freedom is a cry for the possibility to grow, to search and find, to finish man."[265]

3) The third important factor in the Christian's scrutiny of the future is the presence in the Church even today of a very strong positive drive and demand toward community.[266] And Sullivan purposely uses the two terms, drive and demand, jointly to signify that the Church must understand herself today "as the locus of the genesis of the new community." The American Church had this opportunity once before, as has been shown earlier on these pages, but failed to utilize it fully owing to lack of flexibility, openness, and appreciation for change. It is also possible that in early American history the situation was not ripe enough to enable clergy and laity to perceive clearly what this drive and demand should effect, in forms of change, on the local and diocesan level of Church life.

Today the imperative is so clearly spelled out that only a positive, constructive response to the needs of the new community would satisfy those who still place their hope in the Church. For if the Church fails again in placing community ahead of institution, "the Church will write her irrelevancy large for all to read." Sullivan is remarkable in noticing that the response itself to the need is more important than any of its particular forms. He does not favor a "therapeutic community" over an "apocalyptic community" or vice versa. He is convinced that, probably, both elements will be present in a true community. Consequently, he can write with confidence and conviction that the "Catholicism of the year 2000 will be judged–or will have been judged– by its response to this challenge."[267]

Though Sullivan has restricted his considerations of

the future to what he characterizes as the "three vectors" of American Catholic life, i.e., authority, freedom, and community, it is evident that the successful emergence of these vectors on the parish level presupposes and hinges on other factors equally important in the life of the local community for the future. Two of them, as the fourth and fifth factors in future expectations, will be considered here.

4) If it is true that "the future is my present and my world . . . tomorrow,"[268] the fourth factor in future expectations must have something to do with the specifically American character of the local communities. To put it differently, the very conditions of American parishes, as expressions of the human condition here and now, must contribute to a great extent to their theological understanding. The past did not take this requirement seriously. It could not do so owing to the fact that the structural features of Catholic life as well as theological trends and developments were largely imported from Europe. They were not responses sought and elicited by the new American conditions. They were centuries-old traditions and customs, developed as responses to totally different situations and legitimized in the experiences of the Church in Europe.

This statement does not advocate independence for the Church in America from the universal Church nor does it imply any denial of sacred traditions and essential structures. On the contrary, it reaffirms universality in the conviction that the very universality of the Church demands that the particular milieu, values, aspirations, hopes, and traditions of any people to whom the Gospel is proclaimed, be brought into convergence with divine revelation.[269] In this light, it is regrettable and strange

that for many generations American practitioners of theology have looked to Europe for their ideas while ignoring the vital contribution to Christian thought being made in their native land. This indigenous American theology is not merely a 'theology of culture,' as many of its detractors insist, but rather a legitimate expression of the Christian understanding of the gospel.[270]

This positive orientation of American theology toward real human values can contribute greatly to a human approach to the nature of the parish provided that it carefully maintains the balance between the "given" and the failure of man in responding to the given.

5) The fifth factor in the future of the Church in America, and particularly of the American local community, is the predominant role of cybernetics in the present socio-technical society. Expansion of technology in the path of new scientific discoveries in this country has made it possible for man to identify himself with automation and cybernation to such an extent that his own evolution and future seem to be unthinkable without the benefit of his tools and machines. "Any theology which hopes to be of some relevance to these conditions must focus its attention on the problems and promises generated thereby—namely, the man-machine unit of production, the imminent collapse of the Protestant ethic, the ethics of organization, the values of interdependence, the challenge of world unity in an age of technological universality and social plurality."[271]

The theology of the parish is the first in line to feel the good and bad consequences of such a development. And the cybernetic transformation through democratization will be a very significant part of parish life in the future. Out of sheer necessity, it will become a center of communication and control, interacting perfectly and willingly with its environment, countering inertia and listlessness with information and order, and developing and actively promoting the information-conversion process with its input, output, and feedback.[272]

Thus, the cybernetic aspect of the present American culture, together with all the other socio-technological features of the present age, is of paramount importance for the future of the parish. Indeed, it can be affirmed with cer-

tainty that no American parish and "no theological education that fails to understand the blessings and the ills which
technology has brought, or that does not teach men how
to make the best use of its opportunities and at the same
time to free themselves from bondage to it, is likely to
mediate the good news of man's salvation."[273]

The Present Leading from the Past into the Future

The past leads into the future through the experiences
and toil of the present. Itself rooted in and born of the past,
at the same time, inspired and fashioned by high hopes,
objectives, and ideals, the present is eminently qualified
to plan and condition the future. The history of the American parishes only validates this initial understanding. The
parish, too, is a creation of the past; it too, is a conditioning
factor in shaping the future of Christian life. What then,
can a theologian say about the present of the American
parish at a time when courage and fear, hope and despair,
optimism and resignation cloud his vision and push him
into other fields of investigation?

First of all, he should remember W. A. Visser't Hooft's
words that "the confrontation with neopaganism is not only
a frightening challenge but also a magnificent opportunity.
For this confrontation forces us to proceed to a great spring
cleaning, to a purification of the message we have given
to the world, to a ressourcement, throwing us back on the
never-adequately discovered riches of the original Revelation."[274]

Second, to utilize this magnificent opportunity, the theologian must proceed systematically toward dealing with
the thorny questions of the contemporary parish, and pay
his due to both the original message of revelation and the
human condition to which it must address itself. Following
this pattern, it is fitting that the five factors responsible for
the portrait of the American parish of the future be ex-
plored here in their relationship to the present.

Their order, however, will be slightly altered. In keeping with the basic pattern of this entire study, namely, the fundamental interrelationship of revelation and the human condition, the genesis of the community will be dealt with first. It is here that elements of revelation display their formative role. Then the implications of the metamorphosis of authority will be drawn out. Finally, freedom will be examined from the viewpoint of man as mediated and mediating. While in these considerations revelation will always be present as the guiding light of the investigations, reflections on the human condition will gain prominence in dealing with what is specifically American in the parish and in its cybernetic dimension.

The American Parish as a Community

As has been demonstrated on earlier pages, an ecclesial community always depends, by its very nature, on the two vivifying factors of the Word of God and the Eucharist. The American parish is no exception. It is in the interaction of these two factors that community is created. Community, not as a finished product but as a communion in process; a communion that is being generated by personal involvement and interpersonal relationships; a communion to which people are anxious to belong because they know that it is in belonging that their deepest yearnings to be recognized and to grow as persons are fulfilled.

Do the liturgical gatherings of the present American parishes create a sense of community among those who do care to participate? Are the Word of God and the celebration of the Eucharist essential factors in the sense of community?

Bishop John L. May of Mobile, Alabama, dealing with the subject of the proclamation of the Word of God, has answered these questions by clearly establishing the relationship between failure in preaching and the crisis in faith.[275] The implication of the relationship is that poor preaching might be considered as the one single factor most responsible for the lack of interest in the work of the local community.

He discusses two kinds of preaching: the Greeks' style of classical rhetoric based on syntax, arrangement of ideas, and delivery; unfortunately, "too many speakers got the idea that they, or the medium, were more important than the message." He recognizes the second style as that of the Old Testament prophets, of Jesus Christ, the apostles, and their successors, and he calls it "familiar conversation" or homily. It can also be described as a "free and artless discourse."[276]

Evidently, Bishop May favors a balanced view of the two as the best solution of the pressing contemporary problem. For, while there might have been abuses of the Greek style in the past, in the present it is the primitiveness of the homilies which seems to be mainly responsible for the alienation of many from the local ecclesial celebrations. As he puts it: "Our posture and our half-apologetic words are quick to convince our listeners that we know next to nothing. True, this does not generally arouse antagonism. What it does bring forth, all the evidence makes clear, is indifference."[277]

How to counteract such an uncomplimentary situation? How to overcome the complacency revealed in statements like this: "Preaching is one of the least important things" priests do?[278] If preaching is unimportant, what counts in the priestly ministry? Is it not one of the ordinary means of salvation? Do not the documents of Vatican II stress the importance of proclaiming the Word of God as necessary for the Christian peoples' steady growth in Christ and for the Christian community to bear witness to the Lord's charity in the world?[279]

All these questions seem to point in one direction: to the lack of understanding the Word of God as a community-forming agent; to the lack of understanding the basic demands of the human condition as they are experienced today; and to the lack of understanding the necessity of joining the two together whenever the Word of God is proclaimed to the community of the listeners. Consequently, the most urgent need to remedy the desperate situation is found in the better preparation for the twofold understanding of the proclamation of those who are called to take upon themselves the ineffable responsibility of speaking in the name of God.

To carry the point a bit further, another element deserves attention in this regard. Though he does not deal directly with the problem of proclaiming the Word of God, Anthony Schillaci does state explicitly that as theologians must create a whole new set of analogies in order to deal effectively with theology and contemporary reality, so also must liturgists. For them, too, "a whole set of symbols and rituals must be developed to maintain basic contact between sacrament and world. For all Christians this means that the style of our contact with God has to change."[280]

The immediate consequence of the above statement is grave yet mandatory not only for the theologian but also for the minister of the Word of God. He, too, must be "a thoroughly contemporary man, one who lives in his culture as part of it, aware of it, and reflecting upon it. Increasingly, theology will work to humanize the environment in the light of revelation. This process cannot be undertaken by men who are the victims of that environment through lack of awareness. It is doubtful that any man today can afford to live at odds with his technology; for a theologian (and the minister of the Word of God) to whom is entrusted the continuing explanation and development of revelation such naiveté is unthinkable."[281]

It is evident that the call is always there to deliver the Lord to the particular community in the midst of which the proclamation takes place. In the present case that particular community happens to be an American local community, troubled with age-old problems and new issues and blessed with unparalleled opportunities and unexpected openings. It can become a new revelation of God to its members if its minister is a person mediated and mediating in proclaiming the Word.

The second consideration of the American parish as a community is concerned with the celebration of the Eucharist. And in view of past experiences and future expectations, the present seems to urge upon the American Christian community a deeper understanding of the role of the culture and environment in which the celebration takes place. In this connection, the following three areas of great importance press for theological reflection and practical solutions.

The first area of concern is the concept of the parish. For it is hardly a disputed question any more that the parochial principle with its rigid application of the territorial or parish-principle is not the only viable approach to the theology of the Eucharistic community. Yet the core-element of the parish, i.e., its placeness, to use the Rahnerian term again, has to be retained in some form or other. Both the application of the incarnational principle and the understanding of human nature require its retention. Placeness and structure belong to the human condition. Life is impossible without them. If they are not present, man creates them in order to function properly and operate communally.

However, placeness is not an absolute value. It is only a condition for easier living. Therefore, other values can easily supersede it. And personal freedom, esteemed very highly in the United States, certainly supersedes it in American parishes. The consequence is that instead of forcing one unified and uniform Eucharistic celebration on the entire parish, a flexible, multiform, experimental approach to the liturgy should be actively promoted for the benefit of the natural units and promising subcommunities.[282]

Marcel Légaut, writing about the "re-formation" of the diocese, states that it also "requires the constitution of small assemblies wherever there are Christians with sufficient depth to form adult communities, that is, communities having their own characteristics and pursuing specific activities, suitably adapted to the possibilities of their members and enabling them to develop interpersonal relationships at the level of their inner and religious life. As true local Churches ... they would be able to renew the celebration of the Lord's Supper. . . ."[283] This is exactly the point at issue that must be resolved to the advantage of the people involved.

The second area of concern has to do with the ministers of those celebrations. How to provide ministers for natural units and subcommunities at a time when vocations are sparse and withdrawals from the ministry still continue? This "how" raises the question whether the time has not come already for serious theological and ecclesiological consideration of a pluriform ministry for the sake of the diversified people of the local communities. It may be that not only the time is ripe but also sheer necessity suggests that the Church turn to middle-aged men, tried and chastised in the fire of life, to bring their rich experiences to the ministry and to share them with those who hunger for an authentic interpretation of the Christ-event.

On this point, it may be of help to introduce an interesting distinction of Légaut's for discussion. In writing about the natural communities and the need of ministers to take care of them he makes a fundamental distinction between the cultural function, identified with the celebration of the Lord's Supper, and the apostolic mission which summons the apostle, through his presence in word and example, to make Jesus Christ real and actual. Then, he adds the following remark:

> For if the cultural function calls for faith and piety, it does not essentially require the formation, the culture, the spiritual life or, above all, the relatively rare charism that ordains a man to the apostolic ministry. The powers required to fulfill the cultural function could even now be entrusted to a carefully selected number of believers who, having been judged competent and worthy, would have been led before-

hand to regard this function as forming part of their personal role in the Church. Having received the necessary powers, but without being obliged to abandon their profession, they could thus renew the celebration of the Lord's Supper with sufficient frequency, even in their own, posssibly very tiny, community. Only thus will the Church be in a position to ensure the service that all her members are entitled to demand of her, regardless of their situation and private circumstances. *Since Christians are everywhere and constantly subject to insidious pressures and overt persecution, especially in the often inhuman conditions of urban life and industry, they must be given every opportunity to gather fraternally in memory of Jesus, as he requested of his disciples before his death.* Clearly this essential condition must be fulfilled if they too are to become his disciples in the twentieth century. Otherwise how could they even remain believers?[284]

Would it be too much to expect the American parish to introduce such an important structural change for the benefit of the contemporary believer and, at the same time, to reinterpret and reformulate the whole idea of pastorship? Different times gave different interpretations to the local community and its relationship with the minister of the Word of God and the Eucharist throughout Christian history. The present period is no exception at all.

If the already-mentioned claim that a generation now lasts about seven years is valid, this makes it mandatory for the ministers to be sensitive and also critically receptive to things and persons that bring about change. The present legal concept of the ministry and pastorship hardly favors such an approach. For how could sensitivity to causes and reasons of a continuously changing society be maintained in a legal system that expects critical responsibility and creativity from the declining years of the minister?[285]

The third area of concern is the time of the Eucharistic celebration. Though clearly established by early history and always supported by uninterrupted tradition, the Sunday celebration is not the only solution to participation in the community's Eucharistic celebration. The human condition of the present socio-technological era clearly requests other alternatives and a more flexible approach to the whole problem. Such a change might become a simple necessity in the case of decentralization of the parish in favor of the natural subcommunities. A change in policy would not negate the Sunday celebration, but it would not make it exclusive either.

The American Parish as a Seedbed of Collegial Authority

Sullivan's observation on the democratic metamorphosis of authority prompts two remarks. The first is related to the nature of pastoral theology, the discipline preparing and conditioning the candidates for the ministry and particularly for their dealing with people. Such a discipline is based on actual parish life, the lived conditions of flesh and blood communities, and not classroom theorizing alone. From the point of view of quality, it is an intellectual and systematically construed science, without the pretensions, however, of a purely academic and uninvolved attitude.

Consequently, it should be the result of a cooperative effort on the part of excellent pastors, theologians, social scientists, and other professionals.[286] Such a pastoral teamwork theology will deal, from its very start, with both dimensions of the parish: the divine and the human, and will condition future or actual ministers to deal with individuals and communities in the spirit of Christian service and basic democratic equality. Without such a solid foundation one can hardly hope for the complete disappearance of the unbiblical lording over the faithful.

The second remark goes to the very core of the problem by raising the question whether a transition from the past understanding of authority to its collegial exercise is possible at all. When Martin E. Marty and his associates were asked to write a book on the American parish, they held a debate among themselves about what the parish needed to be saved: a "radical surgery" or "a band-aid" treatment. Because they found the parish deadly sick with a cancer, they decided in favor of the radical surgery, and to indicate it, they titled their book *Death and Birth of the Parish*. They also indicated that to bring about the birth of the parish after the surgery, patient attention to detail was needed: "the detail of the Scripture, Christian history, our culture, and modern modes of ministry. Expectation of a miraculous cure was out of the question."

It is helpful to remember on this point that the detail of authority in the form of the human touch working through dialogic consultation and collegial decision-making is one of the elements that has emerged in the consciousness of the contemporary Christian. To get hold of this, radical surgery might be required sometimes to free the communities from structural elements that would only perpetuate the old concept of authority and prevent the metamorphosis from taking place in line with contemporary consciousness. Ministers of the Word and the Eucharist should be the first ones to remember that

> as a structural characteristic of mature adulthood existential authority is not something we possess or something which originates in our controlling or objectifying attitude, it is not an object or a thing. Existential authority is something inspirational and overwhelming, something which originates in our primordial enthusiasm. In the language of Heidegger: man never possesses existential authority. It is existential authority that possesses man. Existential authority creates openness, respect and initiative, and reveals man as a unique representative of the cosmos. And in this sense every mature adult *is* authority over every adult simply by being himself. For as Paul Tillich says, "everyone contributes in a unique

way to the whole. And this unique experience gives, even to the least educated man, some authority over the highest educated one."[287]

The American parish will render an enormous service to mankind and the universal Church by actively promoting the metamorphosis of authority as a deep reverence for man as man.

The American Parish as a Seedbed of Personal Religious Freedom

Nowhere is greater theological and pastoral effort needed than in the parish to explore all the implications of personal religious freedom as they might affect both the life of Christian individuals and the life of their local religious community. If bishops, pastors, and theologians pay only lip service to the greatly changed human condition without wholeheartedly embracing and supporting it as a God-given and God-intended source of religious reflection, one can hardly hope for a true and successful rebirth of the parish.[288] Two areas are particularly outstanding where change in theological and structural trends is necessary to pour new life into the local community.

1) The first area is the sincere and respectful acceptance of the fundamental option as an essential datum of the human person. Life is always torn between the two poles of a human personality: striving to preserve our identity, on the one hand, and appropriating to ourselves the reality in the midst of which we live, on the other. This whole movement involves and demands an unceasing dialogue between a human person and the whole complex reality around him, between the appeals and the responses, between invitations to act and the free responses given to those invitations.

The consequence of this high voltage movement is rather enormous, for it means that the relationship of the appealing, inviting reality and the knowing-appreciating-responding free agent can hardly ever be stabilized and finalized.

It goes, then, without saying that the most crucial step taken by any man is to opt for a basic fundamental view of the whole of reality, grasping the entire spectrum of its values, and to do so freely and honestly, committing himself without reserve to an unceasing dialogue with it, as well as to the maturing process of his own personality as the most outstanding result of the same dialogue. By making such a fundamental option, man looks beyond the immediately available concrete values of his life and intends to concretize them in such a way that his fundamental view of the whole reality would gain due recognition in them.

This recognition could mean either of two things: it could strengthen the option in its original form and scope or it could force man to reconsider and even alter it in view of new data resulting from the ongoing dialogue. For such a fundamental stand towards the whole reality can never become an accomplished fact—in the sense of a static, completed concept of it. The outcome of the dialogue remains a lifetime task to be realized anew every day and in every new act of the human person. What is final is the fundamental commitment to the view of the whole reality.[289]

2) The application of the principle of the fundamental option makes certain shifts inevitable for the contemporary local community.

a) The present understanding of sacramental marriage invites reinterpretation and reformulation. For it is at least questionable that the mere application of the legal form of the marriage ceremony, approved and sanctioned by the Church, between two baptized persons *automatically* creates a sacramental and indissoluble union between them. Though the parties involved are the ministers of the sacrament, it could very well be in these modern days of doubt and denial that they do not even believe in the sacramental nature of marriage. Should not rather sacramental marriage be reserved as a privilege for those who in their marriage union have already proven themselves worthy of being the incarnational expression of Christ's love for His Church?[290]

b) The initiative belongs to the Church in the United States to seek and institute salutary changes and procedures that would bring spiritual relief and comfort to those who, through no fault of their own, have become victims of abuse, infidelity, desertion, and broken marriages. These unfortunate people should be given another opportunity to work out their new fundamental option in accordance with the essentially altered reality, their life-long partner of the dialogue. The ministers of God should be the first to remember that the initial "step in the study of man's relation to God is the study of man in the many-faceted web of his own existence. For God speaks to him and seeks him in that condition instead of in an imaginary abstract world univocally applicable to all men."[291]

In this way, man will not disappear from view under the overemphasis on God's sovereignty and the Church's fascination with divine claims. On the contrary, man will be revered as the mediated and mediating agent of the God-intended and God-given reality whom not even the Almighty would reject because he had to alter his initial fundamental option.

c) In dealing with personal religious freedom on the level of the believing local community, the assistance of the Holy Spirit should also be allowed to play its part. And it might be suggested that because this assistance is neither revelation nor inspiration, it is basically a theological device for the Spirit's operation in and through the believing community. Assistance is given precisely in the convictions, the beliefs, and the growing consciousness of issues as they are registered, experienced, and expressed in the community of believers.

"Consequently, instead of being edicts to be obeyed, the expressions of the ordinary magisterium function so as to bring about more effectively an intensified awareness of specific problems. Otherwise said, the magisterium functions to elicit community consciousness rather than to enforce conformity to directives."[292] A more receptive listening to the Spirit would certainly help solve the problems that fall so heavily on the individual conscience.

The American Parish as a Pluralistic Reality and Center of Communication

If the question is raised as to what is specifically American in the structure of the local church-community, the answer can only point to nothing more and nothing less than a sincere and deep commitment to and wholehearted acceptance of whatever might emerge in the growing consciousness as genuinely human. For as soon as the present diaspora-situation of the Church is clearly recognized, her role as sign and symbol gains prominence primarily in the human dimension of Christian existence. The reason is simple: it is on this level that man initially seeks and finds God today.

It is on this level that the Word of God and the celebration of the Eucharist are responses to the utterly human yet always transcendent dimension which molds and shapes human existence. Consequently, "the parish, in its structure, mentality, piety, and mission must correspond to the essential interdependence of life as it is in God's world."[293] Correspondence, however, is not merely tolerance; it means active seeking of harmony and mutuality.

Furthermore, America is a multi-faceted, pluralistic reality where everybody needs everybody else for the pulsating life of the country. It is so even in the life of the parish, because the American parish, too, is basically pluralistic in nature. This is true not only on the basis of age, education, culture, occupation, wealth, etc., but also and chiefly on the basis of the simultaneous presence of believers and practical unbelievers in its midst.

To reach such people, the minister should enjoy freedom and trust in exploring new possibilities and in experimenting with new structures. Without such a positive step, it might happen that even at this time of rapid changes the American parish will serve and be restricted to those alone who hardly need ministering to their needs.[294] The lost sheep definitely will be written off for good.

To counteract such complacency, the utilization of American technology as a means of development and growth is an absolute necessity. In this cybernetic age every parish should become a center of information and control. Such information, however, does not mean only or even primarily the communication from above in the form of output; it entails the whole sequence of input, output, and feedback, as well as the legally constituted parish agencies to make the cybernetic operation a successful reality.

In spite of some unfortunate experiences of lay involvement in the decision-making process of the local communities, it is distressing and discouraging to see the wall of resistance, built systematically and untiringly by the clergy, against Parish Councils, Parish Boards or Central Committees, etc. Such a short-sighted attitude is no reflection of the laity's inability to participate responsibly in the affairs of the parish. It is a clear though tacit admission of the pastor's inability to work systematically and consistently with others for the benefit of the local people of God.

EPILOGUE

John Ramon Mason, appraising Herbert W. Richardson's *Toward an American Theology*, ruminates on the four possible options open to the theologian today: *retreat* from the pressures of critical culture; *reduction* of faith to secular culture; *revulsion* from Christian faith as incapable of being transposed into any meaningful form; and *reconnaissance* as a critical effort toward doing justice to both the Christian heritage and the shape and style of contemporary life. Then, he states that Richardson's study exemplifies the fourth theological option.[295] He could not be more right. And so it is fitting that this study end with a word about Richardson's contemporary intellectus.

The dominant intellectus of our age is relativism of a special brand. It affirms that all judgments bear a socially relative character and tend to eliminate divine transcendence. To counteract it, one needs the faith as the power of reconciliation, *fides reconcilians intellectum,* "which works to unite the many relative perspectives and to thwart conflict."[296]

Nothing expresses better the theology of the parish today than its function of reconciliation of the divine and human in the communal life of its members. All models have this idea at their root and core. Structures might go, forms might change. But this essential purpose of the local be-

lieving community always remains. This is its finality. This
is the one unchanging and unchangeable thing in the actual
encounter of man with God.

FOOTNOTES

[1]D. Szabo, "La paroisse dans la structure écologique de la ville," *Paroisses urbaines—paroisses rurales.* 5e Conférence Internationale de Sociologie Religieuse (Tournai : Casterman, 1958), p. 27.

[2]Cf. J. Homeyer, "The Renewal of the Parish (A Bibliographical Survey)," *The Parish—from Theology to Practice,* edited by H. Rahner, S.J., translated by Robert Kress (Westminster, Maryland: The Newman Press, 1958); C. Floristan, *The Parish—Eucharistic Community,* translated by John F. Byrne (Notre Dame, Ind.: Fides Publishers, Inc., 1964), 208-240; A. Blöchlinger, *The Modern Parish Community,* translated by Geoffrey Stevens (New York: P.J. Kenedy & Sons, 1964),pp. 235-252. It is interesting to know that *paroikía,* in the Old Testament, means living in a foreign land without rights. Israel lived in this way while in Egypt. Later on, the whole history of Israel was looked upon as being foreign to this world. Early Christianity borrowed this interpretation of life and history from Israel and applied it to itself by claiming that the Christian's true home is in heaven. While in this world, he is living away from his home (1 P 1:17). This interpretation of the term prevailed up to the liberation of the Church by Constantine. It follows that in the first centuries of Christianity *paroikía* really meant the local community gathered around the bishop, hence the diocese. Floristan notes pointedly, "In the years following the Edict of Constantine, the Church's situation changed. In a certain accidental sense Christians no longer lived in a foreign land, in *diaspora.* Little by little they began to lose the eschatological meaning that the local *paroikía*-church had for the first Christians and, instead, the juridical idea began to gain ground," *op. cit.,* p. 48.

[3]Cf. L. Nanni, "L'evoluzione storica della Parrocchia," *La scuola cattolica* 81 (1953), pp. 475-544; G. Bardy, "Sur l'origine des paroisses," *Masses ouvrières* 21 (1947), pp. 42-59; 22 (1947), pp. 42-66; C. Floristan, *op. cit.,* pp. 48-53; A. Blöchlinger, *op. cit.,* pp. 42-45.

[4]C. Floristan, *op. cit.,* p. 51; F. J. Schmale, "Kanonie, Seelsorge, Eigenkirche." *Historisches Jahrbuch* 78 (1959), pp. 38-73.

[5]"During the Middle Ages, the only person who corresponds to our present-day parish priest is, paradoxically, the bishop. He was the city's parish priest. Every Sunday he would celebrate Mass surrounded by his clergy. He would reconcile the penitents, preach, instruct the people, and baptize. . . . The temporal was extremely involved in the spiritual, and a bishop would

often become a person of importance in civil life. In Charlemagne's time he was a temporal lord with his own vassals although primarily a pastor, and his administrative work was comparatively restricted. In those days there were no curial offices for diocesan business. Not until the twelfth and thirteenth centuries do we find vicars-general, notaries, secretaries and the like, because it was not until then that the old presbyterium gave place to the cathedral chapter": F. Henry, O.P., "The Priestly Ministry from Its Beginnings to the Present Day," *My Father's Business. A Priest in France*, by G. Michonneau, translated by Edmund Gilpin (New York: Herder and Herder, 1959), pp. 29-30.

⁶Floristan, *op. cit.*, p. 58.

⁷*Ibid.*, p. 61.

⁸To indicate the educational and moral situation of the clergy at the time of the Council of Trent, it is fitting that chapter six of the "Decree Concerning Reform" of the twenty-first session be quoted here. "Since illiterate and incompetent rectors of parochial churches are but little suited for sacred offices, and others by the depravity of their lives corrupt rather than edify, the bishops may, also as delegates of the Apostolic See, give temporarily to such illiterate and incompetent rectors, if otherwise blameless, assistants or vicars, with a portion of the fruits sufficient for their maintenance or provide for them in some other manner, every appeal and exemption being set aside. But those who live a disgraceful and scandalous life, they shall after admonishing them, restrain and punish; and if they should continue to be incorrigible in their wickedness, they shall have the authority to deprive them of their benefices in accordance with the prescriptions of the sacred canons, every exemption and appeal being rejected": H. J. Schroeder, O.P., *Canons and Decrees of the Council of Trent* (St. Louis, Mo.: B. Herder Book Co., 1960), pp. 139-140.

⁹Chapter 13, session 24, *ibid.*, p. 204.

¹⁰Chapter one, session 23, *ibid.*, pp. 164-165; chapter 4, session 24, *ibid.*, pp. 195-196.

¹¹Chapter 4, session 21, *ibid.*, p. 138.

¹²T. L. Bouscaren, S.J. and A. C. Ellis, S.J., *Canon Law. A Text and Commentary* (Milwaukee: The Bruce Publishing Co., 1949), p. 151.

¹³*Ibid.*, p. 189.

¹⁴*Ibid.*, p. 152.

¹⁵*Ibid.*, p. 151.

¹⁶Charles Davis, "The Parish and Theology," *The Clergy Review* 49 (1964), p. 269.

¹⁷Cf. A. Wintersig, "Pfarrei und Mysterium," *Jahrbuch für Liturgie-Wissenschaft* 5 (1925), pp. 136-143 (French translation, "Le Realisme Mystique de la Paroisse," *La Maison-Dieu* 8 (1936), pp. 15-27); J. Pinsk, "Die religiose Wirklichkeit von Kirche, Diözese und Pfarrei," *Der katholische Gedanke* 6 (1933), pp. 337-344; free French translation, "La liturgie et la réalité spirituelle de l'Eglise, du diocèse et de la paroisse," *Les questions liturgiques et paroissiales* 18 (1933), pp. 192-205; M. Schurr, "Die übernaturliche Wirklichkeit der Pfarrei," *Benediktinische Monatschrift* 19 (1937), pp. 81-106 (English translation, "The Parish as a Supernatural Reality," in *Orate Fratres* 12 (1938), pp. 255-260; 311-317; 410-415; 456-459); Yves Congar, O.P., "Mission de la paroisse," *Structures sociales et pastorale paroissiale*.

Congrès de Lille (Paris: Union des Oeuvres Catholiques de France, 1949), pp. 48-68; Cyprian Vagaggini, O.S.B., *Theological Dimensions of the Liturgy*, vol. I, translated by Leonard J. Doyle (Collegeville, Minnesota: The Liturgical Press, 1959); Godfrey Diekmann, O.S.B., *Come, Let Us Worship* (Baltimore, Maryland: Helicon Press, 1961; Evelyn Underhill, *Worship* (New York: Harper and Brothers, Publishers, 1937). See also all the available literature on liturgy, Catholic Action, and the theology of the laity.

[18]Cf. Joseph H. Fichter, S.J., "The Open Parish in an Open Society," *Catholic World* 201 (April, 1967), p. 17.

[19]John Foster, *Requiem for A Parish*. An inquiry into customary practices and procedures in the contemporary parish (Westminster, Maryland: The Newman Press, 1962), p. 11; see also John J. Harmon, "The Parish: When Is It Alive?—When Should It Die?" *Cross Currents* (Fall, 1965), pp. 385-392.

[20]Foster, *op. cit.*, p. 50.

[21]Cf. the works by Wintersig, Pinsk, and Schurr cited in note 17; L. de Coninck, "Les origines actuelles de la théologie pastorale," *Nouvelle Revue Théologique* 86 (1954), pp. 134-141; A. Liégé, O.P., Introduction to French translation of F. X. Arnold, *Serviteurs de la foi* (Tournai, 1957); D. Grasso, "Osservazioni sulla Teologia della Parrocchia," *Gregorianum* 40 (1959), pp. 297-314; A. Blöchlinger, *The Modern Parish Community* (New York: P. J. Kenedy & Sons, 1964), pp. 92ff; C. Floristan, *op. cit.*, p. 92. G. Le Bras introduced new methods for religious sociology in *Histoire des collections canoniques en Occident* (Paris: 1931-1932) and followed this up with four of the most highly regarded works on religious sociology: *Introduction à l'histoire de la pratique religieuse en France* (Paris: P.U.F., 2 vol., 1942, 1945) and *Etudes de sociologie religieuse* (Paris: P.U.F., 2 vol., 1955-1956).

[22]For example, L. de Coninck and A. Liégé, O.P. See previous note.

[23]D. Grasso, *op. cit.*

[24]Blöchlinger, *op. cit.*, p. 150, followed by Davis, who puts it this way: "There is no theology of the parish as such. There is a theology of the local community that exists *de facto* in the context of the parish. There is a theology of the Church, both as a sacramental and hierarchical structure and as an inner reality, the Church which is present and active in the parish. And the parish itself fulfills the theological demand that the Church should embody itself in concrete, social forms adapted to human life. But as a particular concrete institution, the parish is an ecclesiastical creation that is not in itself a proper object of theology" (*op. cit.*, p. 283). O. V. Nell Breuning and L. Siemer also concur for other reasons: see note 50.

[25]Already in a 1961 article, "Theology of the Parish" (*Worship* 38: 421-426), R. E. Moran, C.S.P., noted that further historical research might well show the parish is not so obviously an offshoot of the diocese, which would force Grasso and his followers to adjust their views. The same would be true of Grasso's presupposition that the presbyters of the early Church were subordinate colleagues of the bishop, which has been questioned in recent times. Cf. also C. Floristan, *op. cit.*, pp. 106-107.

[26]Davis, *art. cit.*, p. 283. (see also Grasso, *art. cit.*, p. 305). It is interesting to see how people can draw different conclusions from the same reality. "The parish is a Christian community of an already fixed church; it is a fraction, sui generis, of the diocesan church. The Church always

begins in an area with a diocese, not a parish. The diocese is not born of a combination of several parishes; instead, parishes start to grow out of the newly born diocese made up at first of a single parish. In this sense the diocese is the 'parish in its fullness' just as the bishop is the 'full pastor,' " Floristan, *op. cit.*, p. 155.

[27]Cf. S. J. Kilian, O.F.M., "Fundamental Option: An Essential Datum of the Human Person," *The American Benedictine Review* 21 (1970), pp. 192-202; *idem*, "The Catholic Theologian and Non-Christian Religions," *Thought* 49 (1974), pp. 21-42; H. Nys, O.P., *Le salut sans l'Evangile* (Paris: Editions du Cerf, 1966); *Foundations of Mission Theology*, edited by SEDOS, translated by John Drury (Maryknoll, N. Y.: Orbis Books, 1972); G. H. Anderson and T. F. Stransky, C.S.P. (eds.), *Mission Trends No. 1*. Crucial Issues in Mission Today (New York; Paulist Press, 1974); C. J. Van der Poel, C.S.Sp., *The Search for Human Values* (New York: Paulist Press, 1971); R. Haughton, *The Theology of Experience* (New York: Newman Press, 1972).

[28]Blöchlinger, *op. cit.*, pp. 147ff; Grasso, *art. cit.*, p. 311.

[29]Henri de Lubac, S.J., makes a clear distinction between particular church and local church, identifying the former with the diocese and the latter with the parish, and he claims that it was the intention of the fathers of Vatican II to favor such a distinction. Cf. *Les églises particulières dans l'Eglise universelle* (Paris: Aubier Montaigne, 1971), pp. 29-56.

[30]W. M. Abbott, S.J. (ed.), *Documents of Vatican II* (New York: Herder and Herder, Association Press, 1966), pp. 152-153.

[31]LG, no. 26; Abbott, *op. cit.*, p. 50.

[32]Ibid.

[33]Abbott, *op. cit.*, p. 418.

[34]Ibid.

[35]In spite of new institutions, such as the permanent diaconate, extraordinary ministers of the Eucharist, and parish councils, the face of the parishes did not change much in the years that have followed the Council. The institution of parish councils has fared particularly badly. The clergy usually find excuses for not having or for suppressing it in the condition of the lay people. They were not trained in ecclesial matters; therefore, they cannot be expected to understand the fine art of ecclesial business. Actually, such convictions indicate a deep-seated though, very often, subconscious fear of the educated laity. As businessmen, the latter are used to a methodical approach to things. They cannot tolerate ad hoc decisions. They expect their priests to know this and proceed accordingly.

[36]CD, no. 31; Abbott, *op. cit.*, p. 419.

[37]Ibid.

[38]LG, no. 8; Abbott, *op. cit.*, p. 22.

[39]B. Kloppenburg, O.F.M., *The Ecclesiology of Vatican II*, translated by Matthew J. O'Connell (Chicago: Franciscan Herald Press, 1974), p. XV.

[40]LG, no. 1; Abbott, *op. cit.*, p. 15; SC, no. 26; Abbott, *op. cit.*, p. 147.

[41]Kloppenburg, *op. cit.*, p. XV.

[42]Davis, *art. cit.*, p. 280.

[43]Ibid. It seems, furthermore, nonsensical to make a distinction "between the supernatural reality *in* the parish and the parish itself in the canonical sense, and between a theology of that supernatural reality, which is not

essentially bound to the parish, and a theology of the parish" (p. 282). The latter simply cannot be without the former. At least, not theologically. Even the most canonical of all canonists must admit that without the theological content the parish would simply cease to be a "parish" of the universal Church. It would be an anomaly. The fact that, before the parish-system was established, *paroikía* and diocese had been used interchangeably for the city-parish-diocese seems to make our point clear. This writer is working on the theology of the local church and will be able to say more on the subject there.

[44]Foster, *op. cit.*, p. 32.

[45]Cf. note 17 above.

[46]Wintersig, *art. cit.*, p. 16.

[47]*Ibid.*, pp. 19-21.

[48]P. Parsch, "Die Pfarre als Mysterium," *Die legendige Pfarrgemeinde*, the Vienna Congress of 1933 (1934), p. 14.

[40]Schurr, p. 84; English translation in Blöchlinger, *op. cit.*, pp. 124-125.

[50]"Pfarrgemeinde, Pfarrfamilie, Pfarrprinzip," *Trierer Theologische Zeitschrift*, 56 (1947), p. 258. L. Siemer represented a similar view by taking a strong stand against the parish as an *ecclesiola*. Cf. "Pfarrfamilie und Ecclesiola," *Die neue Ordnung* 3 (1949), pp. 37-51.

[51]H. Godin and M. Ward, *France Pagan?* (New York 1949).

[52]*Revolution in a City Parish* (Westminster, Maryland: The Newman Press, 1949): *My Father's Business*, translated by Edmund Gilpin (New York: Herder and Herder, 1959); *Pas de vie chrétienne sans communauté* (Paris: Editions du Cerf, 1960).

[53]"Quelques réflexions sur la paroisse," *La Maison-Dieu* 9 (1947), pp. 104-112.

[54]*Revolution in a City Parish*, p. 1.

[55]He delivered an address, "Mission de la paroisse," at the 63rd Còngrès National del'Union des Oeuvres at Lille, France in 1948. It was hailed as an important positive effort toward a theology of the parish. Together with other addresses it was published in *Structures sociales et pastorale paroissiale* (Paris: Union des Oeuvres Catholiques de France, 1949).

[56]*Ibid.*, p. 50.

[57]"*Cette structure, c'est le groupement naturel d'un certain nombre de familles indépendantes, dans la solidarité du quotidien de l'existence*," p. 51.

[58]In reference to Congar's address, Davis notes on page 274 that he has not seen the text himself and is relying on the account given in Blöchlinger, *op. cit.*, pp. 183-192. This is probably the reason why he uses "State," most of the time, for Congar's "cité."

[59]Davis, *art. cit.*, pp. 274-275.

[60]Congar, *op. cit.*, p. 51.

[61]*Divided Christendom* (London: The Centenary Press, 1939), p. 48; *Vraie et fausse reforme dans l'Eglise* (Paris: Editions du Cerf, 1952), p. 95.

[62]See note 55.

[63]Congar, *op. cit.*, pp. 59-60.

[64]*Ibid.*, p. 60.

[65]Davis, *art. cit.*, p. 275; Blöchlinger, *op. cit.*, p. 135f.

[66]Davis, *art. cit.*, p. 275; Blöchlinger, *op. cit.*, p. 135.

[67]Davis, *art. cit.*, p. 276; Blöchlinger, *op. cit.*, p. 137.

[68]Davis, *art. cit.*, p. 277; Blöchlinger, *op. cit.*, p. 137ff.

[69]*The Christian Commitment.* Essays in Pastoral Theology, translated by
Cecily Hastings (New York: Sheed and Ward, 1963), p. 22; cf. also "The
Teaching of Vatican II on the Church and the future reality of Christian
Life," *The Christian of the Future,* translated by W. J. O'Hara (New York:
Herder and Herder, 1967), pp. 77-101; "On the Presence of Christ in the
Diaspora Community according to the Teaching of the Second Vatican
Council," *Theological Investigations,* vol. X (New York: Herder & Herder,
1973), pp. 84-102.

[70]*Ibid.,* p. 23.
[71]*Ibid.*
[72]*Ibid.,* pp. 23-24.
[73]*Ibid.,* p. 24.
[74]*Ibid.*
[75]*Ibid.,* pp. 25-26.
[76]*Ibia.,* pp. 27-37.
[77]*Ibid.,* pp. 32-33.
[78]Cf., for example, "Peaceful Reflections on the parochial principle,"
Theological Investigations, Vol. II. Man In the Church, translated by Karl-H.
Kruger (Baltimore: Helicon Press, 1963), pp. 283-318.; *Theology of Pastoral
Action,* translated by W. J. O'Hara and adapted to an English-speaking audience by D. Morrissey, O.P. (New York: Herder and Herder, 1968); *Theological Investigations,* Vol. X, translated by David Bourke (New York: Herder
and Herder, 1973); "Theology of the Parish," *The Parish—from Theology to
Practice,* edited by Hugo Rahner, S.J., translated by Robert Kress (Westminster, Maryland: The Newman Press, 1958), pp. 23-35.

[79]"Theology of the Parish," p. 24.
[80]*Ibid.,* p. 25.
[81]*Ibid.*
[82]*Ibid.,* pp. 28-29.
[83]*Ibid.,* p. 30.
[84]*Ibid.,* p. 31.
[85]*Ibid.*
[86]*Ibid.,* p. 32.
[87]*Ibid.,* p. 33.
[88]*Ibid.* In his study of the parochial principle, Rahner is anxious to note
that any exclusive application of the parochial principle is impossible. Extra-
parochial and/or supra-parochial structures are always possible, many times
even necessary for the care of souls. Differences in profession, social position,
age, language, sex, etc. could easily necessitate such structures. He supports
these reasons by formulating two additional principles, i.e., the "social differ-
ential principle" and the "free-group principle." He also illustrates the
validity of these principles by what has happened in history so far. Cf.
Theological Investigations, Vol. II, pp. 299, 306ff.

[89]Davis, *art. cit.,* p. 279; Blöchlinger, *op. cit.,* p. 142.
[90]Davis, *art. cit.,* p. 280; Blöchlinger, *op. cit.,* p. 143.
[91]Davis, *art. cit.,* p. 280; Blöchlinger, *op. cit.,* p. 169f.
[92]*Theology of Pastoral Action,* pp. 103 and 101.
[93]*Ibid.,* p. 82.
[94]*Ibid.,* p. 100.

95*Ibid.*, p. 103-104; cf. also *Theology for Renewal—Bishops, Priests, Laity,* translated by Cecily Hastings and Richard Strachan (New York: Sheed and Ward, 1964); *Theological Investigations,* Vol. X, translated by David Bourke, part I (New York, Herder and Herder, 1973).

96*The Parish—Eucharistic Community,* translated by John F. Byrne (Notre Dame, Indiana: Fides Publishers, Inc., 1964).

97*Ibid.*, p. 83.

98*Ibid.*, p. 79.

99*Ibid.*, p. 116.

100*Ibid.*, pp. 116-117.

101*Ibid.*, pp. 117-133.

102*Ibid.*, p. 178.

103*The Modern Parish Community,* translated by G. Stevens (New York: P. J. Kenedy & Sons, 1964).

104Together with Davis, and Grasso to some extent.

105"Pfarrgemeinde, Pfarrfamilie, Pfarrprinzip," *Trierer Theologische Zeitschrift* 56 (1947), pp. 81-106.

106*Ibid.*, p. 150.

107*Ibid.*

108*Ibid.*, p. 159.

109*Ibid.*, p. 233.

110Cf. note 27 above; it is only natural that the importance of the human condition might be overstressed from time to time, and man has to be called back to the meaning and reality of God. Eventually, the process works both ways: to and away from God. Experiencing the human is, however, always involved. And it is not the experience, but its interpretation by man that might turn him away from God. As an interesting illustration of this point, it should be recalled that in March and April of 1976 Malcolm Muggeridge, a British journalist and historian, hosted a six-part TV series, called "A Third Testament." It was designed to represent the comprehension of the human condition in the light of the millenia since the first Testaments were written. Muggeridge chose six men of faith as the writers of this "third testament." To quote him, "When I first became interested in the subjects of this Third Testament—St. Augustine, Blaise Pascal, William Blake, Soren Kierkegaard, Leo Tolstoy, and Dietrich Bonhoeffer—I saw them separately . . . as six characters in search of God. Thinking about them it became clear to me that, though they were all quintessentially men of their time, they had in common a special role—to relate their time to eternity. . . . This has to be done every so often. Otherwise, we forget that, when the lure of self-sufficiency proves too strong, or despair too overwhelming, people need to be called back to God to rediscover humility and with it hope." The series began with St. Augustine. "Thanks largely to (St. Augustine), the light of the New Testament did not go out with Rome's; it remained amidst the debris of the fallen Empire to light the way to another civilization—Christendom—whose legatees we are. It seems that he had been specially groomed for the task—tempered in the fires of his own sensuality, toughened by his arduous explorations of the age's many heresies." Very fittingly, Muggeridge ends "A Third Testament" where it began—"with an earthly city in flames and a social order collapsing. Instead of a professor of rhetoric who became bishop, we have a Lutheran pastor—Bonhoeffer. In his cell the theologian became a mystic, the pastor became a martyr, and the teacher produced his *Letters and Papers from Prison*, one of the great classics of Christian literature" ("A Third Testament," *Cultural Information Service*, March, 1976, p. 7.). See also, "Interplay: Christian Entrepreneurship. An Interview with Alan Green," *ibid.*, pp. 1-4.

111*The Modern Parish Community*, p. 171.

112*The Parish—Eucharistic Community*, p. 115.

113S. J. Kilian, O.F.M., "The Catholic Theologian and Non-Christian Religions," *Thought*, 49 (1974), p. 26.

114No. 11; Abbott, *op. cit.*, p. 209.

115*Ibid.*; see also no. 42; Abbott, *op. cit.*, p. 242.

116No. 12; Abbott, *op. cit.*, p. 211; also, no. 25; Abbott, *op. cit.*, p. 224.

117No. 22; Abbott, *op. cit.*, p. 220-221; also, no. 32; Abbott, *op. cit.*, pp. 230-231.

118No. 1; Abbott, *op. cit.*, pp. 660-661.

119Decree on the Missionary Activity of the Church, no. 8; Abbott, *op. cit.*, p. 594; cf. also *LG*, nos. 16-17; Abbott, *op. cit.*, pp. 34-37; no. 22 of the Decree on the Missionary Activity of the Church deserves a partial quotation here. "The seed which is the Word of God sprouts from the good ground watered by divine dew. From this ground the seed draws nourishing elements which it transforms and assimilates into itself. Finally it bears much fruit. Thus, in imitation of the plan of the Incarnation, the young Churches, rooted in Christ and built up on the foundation of the apostles, take to themselves in a wonderful exchange all the riches of the nations which were given to Christ as an inheritance (cf. Ps 2:8). From the customs and traditions of their people, from their wisdom and learning, from their arts and sciences, these Churches borrow all those things which can contribute to the glory of their Creator, the revelation of the Savior's grace, or the proper arrangement of Christian life.

"If this goal is to be achieved, theological investigation must necessarily be stirred up in each major socio-cultural area, as it is called. In this way, under the light of the tradition of the universal Church, a fresh scrutiny will be brought to bear on the deeds and words which God has made known, which have been consigned to sacred Scripture, and which have been unfolded by the Church Fathers and the teaching authority of the Church.

"Thus it will be more clearly seen in what ways faith can seek for understanding in the philosophy and wisdom of these peoples. A better view will be gained of how their customs, outlook on life, and social order can be reconciled with the manner of living taught by divine revelation. As a result, avenues will be opened for a more profound adaptation in the whole area of Christian life. Thanks to such a procedure, every appearance of syncretism and of false particularism can be excluded, and Christian life can be accommodated to the genius and the disposition of each culture" (Abbott, *op. cit.*, pp. 612-613).

120Cf., for example, H. Nys, O.P., *op. cit.;* Juan Luis Segundo, S.J., *The Community Called Church* and *Grace and the Human Condition*, vols. 1 and 2 of A Theology for Artisans of a New Humanity (Maryknoll, N. Y.: Orbis Books, 1973); Francisco Bravo, *The Parish of San Miguelito in Panama* (Cuernavaca, Mexico: CIDOC, 1966); James O'Gara (ed.), *The Postconciliar Parish* (New York: P. J. Kenedy & Sons, 1967).

121Kilian, "The Catholic Theologian. . . ." p. 27.

122The reader is warned here not to confuse human condition as a vehicle of theological thought with any kind of "humanism." Cardinal John Wright in his article, "The Difficulty of Being Eminently Human in the Face of Contemporary 'Humanism'," *L'Osservatore Romano*, March 4, 1976, pp. 6-7 and 12, did not help the situation at all. The following quote will show the reader why. "Sometimes the rationalizing process uses the traditional vocabulary of religious humanism (as did the earlier Modernists), if only for forensic reasons. Sometimes it adapts the jargon of sociology, psychiatry or politics (democracy today, fascism yesterday, collectivism tomorrow), to give the act a 'Grabber.' Sometimes with greater inventiveness, it devises a vocabulary all its own (Teilhard?), to show the ineffable mystic and cosmic complexity of it all. But the net result is the same: the *person* becomes lost in the ideological shuffle, God ceases to be transcendent and absolute, man becomes a cog in the machinery and Christ a *douce chimère* in the dictatorship and a constitutional deity in the democracies. You pay your taxes and you're assigned your choice" (p. 6.).

123Cf. Kilian, "The Catholic Theologian. . . ." p. 27. Archbishop Giovanni Benelli delivered a homily at the inauguration of the new theological faculty at Abiojan, Ivory Coast, Africa on February 14, 1976. Speaking on African theology, he expressed his hope that Christ's eternal message would be presented to Africa "in a way that is in conformity with the outlook, the culture, and the genius of its people" (*L'Osservatore Romano*, March 4, 1976, p. 12.).

124S. J. Kilian, O.F.M., "Fundamental Option: An Essential Datum of the Human Person," *The American Benedictine Review* 21 (1970), p. 195.

125The colloquium was held at Bologna, at the invitation of Professor Giuseppe Alberigo, in April, 1973, under the auspices of the Académie des Sciences religieuses (Bruxelles). The studies presented there were published by Istina a year later: *La portée de l'Eglise des apôtres pour l'Eglise d'aujourd'hui*. Colloque OEcuménique de Bologne (10-13 avril 1973) (Bruxelles: Office International de Librairie, 1974). The presentations and subsequent discussions isolated some main themes, the very first of which being the normative nature of the Church of the apostles. Istina spells it out as "Conformity to the Gospel, to the deposit, and it is the profound source of the unity of the Church; the doxology, hymnology, the confession of faith, the unity of the community are the elements determining this fundamental unity which has its origin in and is modeled by the Mother-Church of Jerusalem." But a second question also emerged and was concerned with Church-institution. It can, perhaps, be formulated in question-form in this way: "Did it not look 'necessary' to the Christians of Greek culture to detach themselves from the Jerusalem community and to experiment with new forms of ministry?" (*Ibid.*, pp. 3-5). This experimentation betrays an effort toward dealing with the human condition very early in the life of the Church.

126J. D. Zizioulas, "La continuité avec les origines apostoliques dans la conscience théologique des Eglises orthodoxes," *La portée de l'Eglise des apôtres pour l'Eglise d'aujourd'hui*, pp. 65-94. The study has also been published in English, "Apostolic Continuity and Orthodox Theology: Towards a Synthesis of Two Perspectives," *St. Vladimir's Theological Quarterly*

(1975), pp. 75-108. Whenever we quote the article we will refer to this **English text.**

127The reader might object to some of the thoughts presented here, and particularly to the details of the study of Zizioulas. It seems important to deal with it because of its understanding of the necessity of having tension in the Church without which its vitality would be lost. He calls it a tension between what is historical and what is eschatological in the Church. We call it the tension between revelation and the human condition that are supposed to be harmonized in the Kingdom of God. Therefore, we limit ourselves only to those aspects of the study that help further the basic ideas of our study. The reader is advised, however, to study the entire article in order to appreciate its beauty and freshness.

We should also call attention to Report No. 13 of the San Miguelito priests in which they state that the divine Word, immanent in all of creation and in man himself, is also clearly discernible and intelligible to men who want to hear it. It is "a call, an order . . . to perfection, and since man is of himself incomplete, and finds his completeness in others, it is a call to union. Men must, therefore, respond to the Immanent Word of God by perfecting themselves, by becoming more and more human, by uniting with others in a truly human fashion. . . ."

We are especially pleased to read in the report the following important statement: "Our first duty, therefore, is to give testimony to the Immanent Word of God which is not the same as what we call the Revealed Word of God. We, more than all the rest, ought to believe in the Immanent Word of God and respect it. We ought to be awfully conscious of the millions of people who, in one way or another, are responding to the Word of God as they understand it in their own nature and in all of creation. We must be convinced that nothing good in this world is profane, because it is a part of that process of perfection and unity. We must be very careful not to violate God's own creation by pretending that the Revealed Word of God alone is valid and real. Thus, for example, all the sciences and activities and movements that spring from man's response to the Immanent Word have a true sacredness of their own, and must not be depreciated by us or confused with the Revealed Word of God.

"Thus every science has a dignity and inviolability of its own—mathematics, sociology, philosophy, history can never be Christian or non-Christian, rather good or bad, true or false . . . human, less human or inhuman . . . So also we ought to respect mightily those men of good will who respond to the Immanent Word of God by devoting themselves to the work of perfecting and uniting the human race, whether it be in universities, the *United Nations,* trade unions, or community development. Any other view would put us in the untenable position of not respecting the Word of God in creation and stating that man is essentially corrupt": Francisco Bravo, *The Parish of San Miguelito in Panama* (Cuernavaca, Mexico: CIDOC, 1966), pp. 432-433.

128Zizioulas, *op. cit.,* pp. 76-77.

129*Ibid.,* pp. 78-79.

130*Ibid.,* p. 87. In the "General Introduction" to the series of *The Library of Constructive Theology* the editors wrote already in 1937: "The conviction that religious experience is to be taken as the starting-point of theological reconstruction does not, of course, imply that we are absolved from the labour of thought. On the contrary, it should serve as the stimulus to thought. No experience can be taken at its face value; it must be criticised and interpreted. . . . Nor do we mean by 'experience' anything less than the whole experience of the human race, so far as it has shared in the Christian consciousness. As Mazzini finely said, 'Tradition and conscience are the two wings given to the human soul to reach the truth'." Evelyn Underhill, *Worship* (New York: Harper & Brothers, 1937), p. IX.

John J. Ryan seems to stress the same point in his "Post-Tribal Worship," when he writes, "The Incarnation means, among other things, that now the 'above' is forever 'below,' eternity has entered time to transform it; the changing things of this world will one day endure forever, transformed in the 'new heaven and new earth.' Nothing of our temporal order is without its enduring significance. Our here-and-now involvements are precisely what in our prayers must be confronted by the eternal," James O'Gara (ed.), *The Postconciliar Parish* (New York: P. J. Kenedy & Sons, 1967), pp. 166-167.

[131]Zizioulas, *op. cit.*, p. 88. Frederick C. Grant, in responding to the Dogmatic Constitution on Divine Revelation (*Dei Verbum*), writes: "The Article rules out the erroneous idea that God is the Great Unknown, not only to all men in general but even to Christians, for it safeguards the sound principle that God has revealed Himself to all men, in nature, in history, and may be known by the light of human reason. This has always been one of the most stable and dependable principles in Catholic theology, and its modern repudiation in some areas of Protestantism has been a major tragedy, whose full consequences are now becoming apparent among those who speak lightly of the 'death of God' and of 'religionless Christianity.' The Christian faith, as many of us believe, reflects the climax of revelation which began long before human history and has been available to all men everywhere (Jn 1:9; Ac 14:17)": Walter M. Abbott, S.J., (ed.), *The Documents of Vatican II*, p. 129.

"The theology of the word on the other hand, while it denies that there is any way from man to God, does claim that God has come to man and has spoken his word. The knowledge of God, inaccessible from man's side because of his finitude and sinfulness, is made available to faith by God's free act of grace. God's word is known in Jesus Christ, to whom the Bible bears witness and whom the Church proclaims in her preaching. Apart from this revelatory word, we can know nothing of God, but in the word God makes himself known to man by his own revelation": John Macquarrie, *Twentieth Century Religious Thought. The Frontiers of Philosophy and Theology*, 1900-1960 (New York: Harper & Row, 1963), p. 319.

Juan Luis Segundo, instead of separating the two ways of revelation, brings them together as he writes: ". . . the relationship between the man of good will and the Christian who was working for the betterment of the world—the one divine vocation of all men—did not simply mean that they were collaborating from their different level of knowledge: one having anonymous, implicit, spontaneous knowledge and the other having precise, explicit, and reflected knowledge. It also meant that this work was the start of faith for the man of good will. It was a journey toward an encounter, the preparation for a dialogue, the gradual formulation of a question that sought, with the ever-growing intensity of love itself, the good news that the Christian had to give." *The Community Called Church*, p. 56.

[132]The reader should be warned not to consider these models in isolation or even as independent of one another. Depending on the intensity of revelation and the cultural and social background of each parish community one of them can prevail over the rest. Basically, however, they represent a sequence of experiences that should take place in each community. Revelation and the human condition should interact continuously, and the predominance of either of them would give the particular characterization of the model most influential in the parish community at a given time. Ideally, these models will lead to one another until the development reaches its climax in the fifth model as the most complete realization of both the divine and the human element in it.

[133]Avery Dulles, S.J., *Models of the Church* (Garden City, N. Y.: Doubleday and Company, Inc., 1974), p. 10. One could ask with James O'Gara: "How should we conceive of the parish? It may be that the early days of the Church offer us a valuable lesson here. For if one is to rely on presently available evidence, variety was then the rule. Different types of structures are reported, depending on the particular needs to be met, or even more significantly, on the sociological factors and cultural patterns encountered. (In the light of current debate over the best means of Christian education, it is interesting to note that as early as the ninth century it was argued that every parish should have a school open to all children and not simply to clerics.)":"Foreword," *The Postconciliar Parish* (New York: P. J. Kenedy & Sons, 1967), p. VIII.

[134]Dulles uses another distinction here when he writes about two types of models in theology: the explanatory and the exploratory. His explanatory models come very close to the exemplary historical model while the exploratory models are supposed to lead to new theological insights. We feel, however, that the exact element that makes them exploratory or heuristic models is not evident at all while in our formulation it is offered clearly in the human condition. Cf. Dulles, *op. cit.*, pp. 22-23. It goes without saying that none of the models should ever be applied in isolation of or in contradistinction to the rest of the models. A healthy parish-community thrives on all of them, though in different degrees and to different extents, always giving prominence to the one or ones which best respond to its particular need, background, culture, etc. Whenever one deals with models, it is dangerous to think in either/or dichotomies or to claim exclusivity for one at the expense of the others.

[135]Hans Urs von Balthasar, "God Has Spoken in Human Language," *The Liturgy and the Word of God* (Collegeville, Minnesota: The Liturgical Press, 1959), p. 35.

[136]*Ibid.*, p. 41.

[137]*Ibid.*, p. 42.

[138]Constitution on the Sacred Liturgy (*SC*), nos. 7 and 33; Abbott, *op. cit.*, pp. 41 and 49.

[139]M. Magrassi, O.S.B., "Tipologia Biblica e Patristica e Liturgia della Parola," *Liturgia della Parola,* Extract from *Rivista Liturgica* 3 (Sept. 1966), p. 55.

[140]For example, J. A. Jungmann, S.J.: "Is this liturgy of the word really a liturgy? It is certainly part of the liturgy in the theological and historico-liturgical sense, in the same sense that the Divine Office was part of the

liturgy for centuries. . . . If nothing else, the liturgy of the word is certainly liturgy by episcopal right.(It is therefore unnecessary to apply the term commonly used in Latin countries, the paraliturgy, to them.)": *The Liturgy of the Word*, translated by H. E. Winstone (Collegeville, Minnesota: The Liturgical Press, 1965), p. 81. He seems to be joined in this view by A. Nocent who maintains that the presence of the Lord in the Celebration of the Divine Office, is neither understood nor accepted by the vast majority: *Célébrer Jésus-Christ, L'Année Liturgique*, vol. I (Paris: Jean-Pierre Delarge, Editeur, 1975), p. 42. A. Bugnini also seems to be of this opinion: see note 142.

141For example, M. Morganti, O.F.M.: "Celebrations [of the Word of God] are neither liturgical actions nor, normally, 'sacred exercises,' but they are simply 'pious exercises'": "Le Sacre Celebrazioni della Parola di Dio," *Liturgia della Parola*, Extract from *Rivista Liturgica* 3 (Sept. 1966), p. 67. He is apparently joined in this opinion by P. Mass, *ibid.*, p. 3. J. Gallen, *Scripture Services* (Collegeville, Minnesota: The Liturgical Press, 1965), p. 3, takes it for granted that Scripture Services are extra-liturgical celebrations while A. Martimort outlines the reasons for this classification, pointing out at the same time their importance as recommended by the Council; he uses this fact to highlight the tenuous character of the line that exists between liturgical actions and "pious exercises": in some cases only the lack of official recognition. Cf. *L'Eglise en Prière. Introduction a la Liturgie* (Paris: Desclee, 1965), p. 9.

142The reason for the dispute is that Vatican II made mention of "liturgical actions" and "pious exercises" in the Constitution on the Sacred Liturgy (no. 13) but carefully refrained from providing a clear criterion for distinguishing the two. Some liturgists, therefore, have recourse to the Instruction of the Sacred Congregation of Rites of September 3, 1958 (no. 1) to obtain this criterion. This Instruction lists five characteristics of liturgical actions. They are sacred actions (1) instituted by Jesus Christ or the Church and (2) are performed in their name (3) by legitimately appointed persons (4) according to liturgical books approved by the Holy See, (5) in order to give due worship to God, the saints, and the blessed. Other sacred acts performed inside or outside the church, even if performed by a priest or in his presence, are called "pious exercises." And it goes without saying that non-liturgical actions possess neither the grace nor the guarantee of the liturgy. Applying these definitions strictly, these authors conclude that Bible Vigils are not liturgical actions.

Others like Jungmann who points out that there has been a change in many places in the Church in the attitude toward Bible Vigils and uses some of the Council's criteria to arrive at their liturgical character. And in truth, it may well be that Jungmann is right despite all the arguments marshalled by those on the other side. In 1965 the Vatican Press published a volume on the liturgical reform entitled *Verso la Riforma Liturgica: Documenti e Sussidi* and the author of the pastoral helps and notes that were added to official documents was none other than A. Bugnini, the leading liturgist who had a hand in many of the reforms themselves. One of his notes reads as follows:"*The sacred celebrations of the Word of God.*One of the most useful didactic means is the celebration of the Word of God modeled after the schema of the Liturgy of the Word of God at Mass. It is the task of Diocesan

Liturgical Commissions to suggest and prepare suitable aids for the dignified and exemplary development of these celebrations which are recommended by the Ecumenical Council (no. 35, no. 4). *Paraliturgies as didactic forms.* Different from Celebrations of the Word of God are paraliturgies. . . ." It would thus appear that Bugnini may be of the opinion that such Celebrations of the Word are liturgical actions.

Be that as it may, what is important for us to remember is that "every supernatural action even when done by an individual person privately, and all the more when although not liturgical it is carried out in common and at the command of the hierarchy, is by some title and to some degree an action of Christ in the Church": C. Vagaggini, *The Commentary on the Constitution and on the Instruction on the Sacred Liturgy,* ed. A. Bugnini and C. Braga, C.M., translated by Vincent Mallon, M.M. (New York: Benziger Bros., 1965), pp. 77-78.

[143]G. Barbaglio, "Iniziazione biblica e Celebrazione della Parola nei Seminari," *Liturgia della Parola,* Extract from *Rivista Liturgica* 3 (Sept. 1966), p. 90.

[144]A. Nocent, O.S.B., *op. cit.,* pp. 43-44.

[145]R. McNally, S.J., Introduction to J. Gallen, S.J., *Scripture Services* (Collegeville, Minnesota: The Liturgical Press, 1963), pp. 4-5.

[146]Decree on Divine Revelation (*DV*), no. 25: Abbott, *op. cit.,* p. 127.

[147]Vatican II, Decree on the Ministry and Life of Priests (*PO*), no. 4: Abbott, *op. cit.,* p. 538 (altered).

[148]"The word of God begets Christian community and it is truly proclaimed and heard only where the Church exists. There are many forms of preaching but they are not authentic unless they correspond to tradition. For this reason, only those witnesses who have received the tradition can indicate what the word of God is and send messengers to announce it. In the local Christian community, born thanks to the strength of the word of God, only those who serve the community in a biblical sense can announce the word so that the community may grow as a Church": C. Floristan, *op. cit.,* p. 33.

[149]Floristan, *ibid.,* p. 49. Then, in reference to the death of Isidore of Seville, the last of the Fathers, Floristan says: "Dissolution of the catechumenate ensued, which in turn caused a devitalization of pastoral activity in that field of Church action, which through the proclaiming of Kerygma, constitutes not only the beginning of the salvific process but also the inseparable sustenance of the eucharistic meal. Since that time forward, a shadowy half-light has obscured the patristic thinking which held that in a certain sense the Christian continues to be a catechumen all his life" (*ibid.,* pp. 49-50).

It is quite possible that one of the main causes of the contemporary Church's troubles is the almost complete absence of the catechumenate from the life of the parish. The Sunday homilies are so wanting in the uttering and proclaiming of the Word of God and so preoccupied with the business-aspect of the local church that the continuous growing of the Christian in awareness of the Word of God and its daily application to the human condition has become only a thing to hope for. This remark is even applicable to the CCD center for children. A new study by the Education Department of the United States Bishops shows that the Church was formerly reaching 77% of potential youngsters with Catholic education, counting both Catholic schools and CCD, whereas presently only 56% are reached. But the saddest part of the situation is the fact that the decline in enrollment in Catholic schools is not countered by a paralleled increase in CCD; consequently, fewer children are being reached by the Church now than before. Does not this reflect a dire need of the Word of God?

150*Op. cit.*, p. 92. Zizioulas is particularly harsh on Orthodox theology, when he writes: "Orthodox theology has not fully drawn its conclusions from this. There is a prevailing view among the so-called 'conservative' Orthodox theologians that the doctrines of the Church constitute something 'untouchable.' This turns dogmas into petrified relics from the past and widens the chasm between the historical and the eschatological perspectives of the continuity of the apostolic kerygma. A study of the early Church and an appreciation of the eucharistic basis of doctrine, however, shows that it is better to understand dogmas as doxological statements of the community, the 'faith transmitted *to the saints*,' in new forms of experience and with a constant openness to the future" (*ibid.*, pp. 93-94).

151Cf. Joseph P. Fitzpatrick, S.J., "Parish of the Future," *America* (Nov. 6, 1965), pp. 521-523. We lean heavily on this article in our presentation of the experiment. See also Francisco Bravo, *The Parish of San Miguelito in Panama* (Cuernavaca, Mexico: CIDOC, 1966). The situation faced by the three American priests was extremely difficult, as they themselves described it in their Report No. 2 to Albert Cardinal Meyer, Archbishop of Chicago, April 6. 1963: "All three of us are coming to the opinion that the present manner of saying Mass for the people may, perhaps, be doing more harm than good. Few, if any, of those who attend have a clue as to what the Eucharist truly means. Worse, the few who do go are almost all women and children—a phenomenon which badly impresses the male portion of the population. We are of the opinion that if we were to start again, it might be wise, from a strategical point of view (if not for pastoral and theological reasons also), to declare a moratorium on Mass, say for a year. This first year would be spent in organizing the community so as to make it naturally 'Christianable' and imparting the Word of God so as to challenge the people to a truly relevant form of Christianity. When formed and ready, the people would give their answer individually and collectively in the Great Act of Thanksgiving which is the Mass" (Bravo, *op. cit.*, p. 348).

152Fitzpatrick, *op. cit.*, p. 521. Leo T. Mahon wrote in Report No. 11 in reference to the priest's obligation to remain faithful to the Word of God: "Every sacrament is an encounter that calls for the taking of an oath. Holy Orders, I submit, is the taking of an oath to form the people of God—to reform the world (nothing less). The priest swears to do it by means of the Word of God. It follows that to the degree that the priest commits himself to the preaching of the Word of God, to that same degree he is faithful to his priesthood; on the other hand, to the degree that the priest departs from the ministry of the Word, to that same degree he abdicates his priesthood. Finally, it is my position that the ministry of the Word of God to real people is the true function of the ordained priest; he it is who, by calling, showing, leading, answering, struggling and working with flesh and blood, builds the Church, the people of God" (Bravo, *op. cit.*, p. 415).

153*Ibid.*, p. 140.

154In their Report No. 2, April 6, 1963, just about five weeks after they had arrived in Panama, they were already able to mention the fact that they enlisted 125 men while only forty men out of 375 persons attended Mass the first Sunday they had celebrated in Panama.

155Fitzpatrick, *op. cit.*, p. 522. Carl E. Braaten, in his *Christ and His Community in the World*, writes pointedly: "I believe now that were I to be pastor again, I would honeycomb the parish with small cells, study groups, meeting once a week. I would spend my time teaching them to be the church, to do what I was spending my time doing in the neighborhood, something they could actually do much more effectively. They would be taught what it means to be a believer in Jesus Christ and a member of His church today. We would discuss how this works itself out in the actual lives of our members. . . . I would rather now work as the communists, indeed as the first Christians did. I would think my first obligation is to minister to those who are already Christians, so that they might become a community, a ministering community in the world" (quoted by Paul R. Biegner in *Death and Birth of the Parish* (St. Louis, Missouri: Concordia, 1964), p. 83.

156Fitzpatrick, *op. cit.*, p. 523. In their Report No. 10 they relate an interesting story: "Recently a Chilean Bishop told us a relevant story. He had been asked to send a priest to a worker area to be its pastor. A young priest, an expert in cooperatives, was assigned there. He worked hard, particularly on cooperatives, and was popular with his people. (Please keep in mind that Chile, despite its enormous problem of poverty is a sophisticated, advanced country.) After six months, a group of workers representing the people went back to the Bishop with the following complaint: 'We asked for a priest. You sent us a cooperativista. We want to hear the Word of God.'

"Panama, like all of Latin America, needs and wants the Word of God. Why, then, does the Church insist on sending teachers, nurses, etc., when the one great necessity—one only we, the missioners, can correspond to—is the Word of God? It is a disturbing phenomenon that a vast percentage of North American missioners in Latin America are teaching English. More, why do we continue to send personnel (priests, Brothers, Sisters, laity) who are not well trained in the Word of God?" (Bravo, *op. cit.*, p. 409).

157*Ibid.*, p. 523.

158*Ibid.*

159The result is a five volume series called *A Theology for Artisans of A New Humanity*. The volumes are: *The Community Called Church, Grace and the Human Condition, Our Idea of God, The Sacraments Today,* and *Evolution and Guilt*. All of them published by Orbis Books, Maryknoll, New York. The first and the second volumes are of special interest to our study. As the series-title indicates, the main objective of the whole enterprise was to build a new humanity; in such an undertaking the historical and the eschatological aspects, revelation and the human condition, do play a preponderant role. Since we can do justice here neither to the methodological value nor to the doctrinal aspect of the series, the reader is strongly urged to study both volumes carefully and to draw his own conclusions concerning the validity of our claim.

160Segundo, *The Community Called Church*, p. VII. The younger generation invoke this argument quite often in justifying giving up the practice of their faith. The remark could be particularly enlightening with respect to the disappointing attitude of many graduates from Catholic schools and colleges.

161*Ibid.* In 1967 I assigned the Pastoral Constitution on the Church in the Modern World to my undergraduates for the first time. I was elated to see a modern approach to the Church and contemporary problems worked out in the document. My students, however, found even this most modern of all documents simply horrifying because of its ornate language and antiquated style.

162*Ibid.*, p. IX. The term "specialized sister theology" is a reference to theology done by scholarly experts while the Segundo- or parish-type-theology is rooted in a faith-in-crisis situation. "Obviously there is no divorce between the two. But it is equally obvious that the former could never serve as the theology for the common run of mortals, whether they be laymen or clergymen. Theology, insofar as it is a scholarly science, will always be the domain of a small minority. Faith, on the other hand, can never be the privileged and exclusive possession of this minority. As the Church sees it, it can be relevant for all men" (*ibid.*, p. VIII).

To do this, a rank and file feedback is absolutely necessary at all times. For the Segundo-group, it took place in the seminars where an hour-long lecture was followed by "a few moments in personal meditation on the questions emerging from the lecture. In this way they can make an effort to formulate a personal solution, however provisional it might be, to the questions posed. . . . In other words, the discussion represents a confrontation between what they have heard and what they have learned from their real-life experiences; between that which they accepted uncritically as children and adolescents and that which they have put together into a coherent whole as adults" (*ibid.*, p. X.). Whenever such confrontation is not made possible institutionally, the conflict will provoke a personal solution in the individual conscience that might well end up in the total alienation of the person involved.

It is very interesting to read some remarks made by the San Miguelito priests on this point in their Report No. 9. "Father Juan Luis *Segundo*, S.J., the famous theologian from Uruguay, has produced a valuable theory on Latin American Catholicism. He states that the Revelation of the Word of God is an unfolding process, not only in the sense of being given by God gradually, but even more importantly in the sense of being understood and assimilated ever so slowly and gradually by the people of God from the time of Abraham to our own. Father *Segundo* further states that the people in Latin America, depending on place, education, class, etc., are in various stages of assimilation of the Word of God. Each people, each area must be studied carefully because it hardly makes sense to attempt to advance a people without knowing the 'terminus a quo.'

"We do not pretend to have done an exhaustive and definitive study of our people, but we believe that we now have a fairly accurate notion of the 'Word' position, the 'terminus a quo' of our people. Father *Segundo* states that there are many people in Latin America who are still in the stage of pre-Christian revelation. In some respects, this is true for our people. To mention two examples: (1) their devotion to the Saints is perilously close to polytheism, definitely a pre-Christian state of revelation; (2) their understanding of and morbid preoccupation with death, surely a pre-Christian state of assimilation of revelation. All one has to do is attend a nine-day wake here (the novenario) to be brought back on the wings of time to the pre-Christian era" (Bravo, *op. cit.*, pp. 383-384). The "terminus a quo," and its inseparable partner the "terminus ad quem," clearly indicate the presence of the historical and the eschatological elements in Segundo's mind.

[163]Bravo, *op. cit.*, p. 11.

[164]*Ibid.*, pp. 24, 25.

[165]*Ibid.*, pp. 27-28; two basic Pauline texts are utilized to indicate these two planes. In Romans 5:15-20 revelation in the human condition is explained, while Ephesians 1:1-10 and 3:1-21 offer beautiful summations of God's revelation in Jesus Christ.

[166]*Ibid.*, pp. 29-30.

[167]*Ibid.*, pp. 72, 73.

[168]*Liturgical Piety* (Notre Dame, Ind.: University of Notre Dame Press, 1955), p. 18.

[169]*Constitution on the Sacred Liturgy* (*SC*), nos. 26-27; Abbott, *op. cit.*, pp. 147-148.

[170]*Ibid.*, no. 47, p. 154.

[171]Cf. "La Messa è un Atto di Culto Risultante da Parola e Eucaristia," *Notitiae 12* (1976), pp. 61-65.

[172]Evelyn Underhill, *Worship* (New York: Harper & Brothers Publishers, 1937), p. 120.

[173]Fitzpatrick, *art. cit.*, p. 522.

[174]Decree on the Ministry and Life of Priests (*PMV*) no. 6; Abbott, *op. cit.*, p. 545. J.-J. von Allmen writes in *Worship: Its Theology And Practice*, p. 42, "that by its worship the Church becomes itself, becomes conscious of itself, and confesses itself as a distinctive entity." He also points out, p. 50: "The Church learns through its cult, and manifests thereby, that it does not exist for itself, and has no justification in itself. It exists—as did the incarnate Christ—for God and for men. Thus it has a twofold orientation."

[175]Joseph M. Powers, S.J., *Eucharistic Theology* (New York: Herder and Herder, 1967), p. 15; he also remarks even in reference to the Roman Mass of the fourth and fifth centuries that "the community itself was the focus of the celebration, this to the extent that in the liturgy of the Roman basilica, the altar itself was only a table brought into the presbyterium when it came time for the Eucharistic prayers and offerings" (p. 26). This role of the community in the first few centuries of Christian history is so clearly perceived today that actually it has become a tremendous incentive in promoting pastoral concern in the liturgical renewal. Cf. J. A. Jungmann, "The People's Part in Mass," *Sacramentum Mundi*, vol. 2, p. 273.

[176]Powers, *op. cit.*, pp. 24-25: "A number of factors contributed to the fact that the Eucharist became a clerical preserve. One factor was the simple matter of language. Out of their esteem for things Roman as signs of authentic culture, the men of the 8th and 9th centuries abhorred translating either the Mass or the scriptures into the now dominant Romance dialects. Thus only the clergy and the educated classes could really understand what the Eucharistic prayers were saying. Further, Isidore of Seville's prevalent sacramental theology presented the sacrament as a 'sacred secret,' a stress which was accented even more by the silence of the canon and many other prayers

of the celebrant. The emphasis on the divinity of Christ and the consequent phenomenon of prayer being addressed to Him, rather than being addressed to the Father through Him, coupled with the frequent protestations of unworthiness, emphasized the Eucharist as the *mysterium tremendum,* and the primitive admonition that 'holy things are for the holy' took on the meaning that the Christian community was itself unworthy of its Eucharist and that the community's place is at a distance from the Eucharistic action. No longer was the Eucharist placed in the hands of the communicants (who, responding logically to the 'apologies' of the liturgy, became fewer and fewer), and when the Eucharist was received, it was received not in the traditional posture of Christian prayer, standing, but in a posture of servility, on one's knees."

177Powers, *op. cit.,* pp. 30-31. How this heritage of medieval piety has affected the mentality of Central America and how it is countered in the San Miguelito community is described very vividly in Report No. 10: "When we arrived here, of course, there was no sense of parish, of Christian community in San Miguelito. Further, the people had never even seen such a phenomenon because there are few, if any, true parishes in the country. . . . Even if a priest knows and is well related to all the people in his area, he still does not have necessarily a true parish. Such involves the combination of a horizontal relationship of people to people as well as the vertical relationship of priest to people. An indication of this fault is seen in the tendency to shy away from the word parish itself. Most churches here are known not as parishes but as Churches or Santuarios dedicated to a special Saint like St. Anthony or Immaculate Heart of Mary. These are centers of individual devotion, and not of community prayer and action. Even the Mass, our central act of worship, is looked upon principally as a suffrage for the dead and not as an assembly of the community united in the Supper of the Lord.

"We now have a hard core of approximately 500 families who live the faith to an astonishing degree—that is, they are a true community. They share one another's joys and sorrows, faith and ideals and what, in short, is most essential, they share a common friendship and trust. They come to Mass now, not as an obligation nor as much to pray for the dead, but rather to meet one another, to sing to one another, to be one in the Lord, to share together the marvelous power of the Word of God and the precious communion of the banquet" (Bravo, *op. cit.,* p. 396).

178Powers, *op. cit.,* p. 95. J.-J. von Allmen does not hesitate to call cult "the criterion of parochial life" for "if the cult ceases the community dies." Actually, "a parochial organization which was indifferent to rooting itself first of all in the cult would be parasitic" (*op. cit.,* p. 55).

179Zizioulas, *art. cit.,* pp. 90-91.

180*Theological Dimensions of the Liturgy,* vol. I, translated by Leonard J. Doyle (Collegeville, Minnesota: The Liturgical Press, 1959), p. 160,

181*Art. cit., Sacramentum Mundi,* p. 273. Cf. Godfrey Diekmann, O.S.B., *Come Let Us Worship* (Baltimore, Maryland: Helicon Press, 1961), pp. 8-21. He writes on page 13: "To put it bluntly: the laity were in practice excluded from actual sharing in the heart of the Sacrifice, as soon as Christ's divinity was over-extolled at the expense of His high-priestly humanity."

182Cf. "Liturgy in the Parish," Hugo Rahner, S.J. (ed.), *The Parish— From Theology to Practice,* p. 67.

Г.

[183]*LG.* no. 23; Abbott, *op. cit.,* p. 44.

[184]*Ibid.,* no. 26; Abbott, *op. cit.,* p. 50.

[185]Cf. N. Afanassieff, "Una sancta," *Irenikon,* 36 (1963), pp. 436-475; A. Asnaghi, "A proposito di Ecclesiologia Eucaristica," *La Scuola Cattolica,* 92 (1964), pp. 443-444; N. Afanassieff, "The Church which Presides in Love," *The Primacy of Peter* (London: Faith, 1963), pp. 57-110; B. Schultze, "Universal or Eucharistic Ecclesiology," *Unitas,* 17 (1965), pp. 87-106, etc.

[186]*The Critic,* June-July, 1966, pp. 32-37.

[187]*Ibid.,* p. 32; he actually refers to the San Miguelito-experiment as the example to be followed. James O'Gara stresses the same idea when he writes in *The Postconciliar Parish,* p. IX: "To my mind the liturgists and the sociologists have made the greatest contribution to our thinking on the parish in recent years. To the liturgist the parish is, or should be, a small-scale reproduction of the mystery of the Church. It is the Church in miniature. In the parish the faithful gather around the altar to communicate with Christ and with one another. In the parish the People of God, priests and people together, form an *ecclesiola,* a Church in small; in the parish the mystery of the Church is realized. The whole congregation, the whole community, offers the Church's sacrifice." Cf. also Joseph T. Nolan, "For Example," *ibid.,* pp. 92-93. Cf. also Richard Currier, *Restructuring The Parish* (Chicago, Illinois: Argus Press, Incorporated, 1967), p. 65.

[188]*The Future Shape of Ministry* (New York: The Seabury Press, 1971), p. 235.

[189]Greeley, *art. cit., p.* 33.

[190]"The Question of the Parish as a Community," *Worship,* XXXVI (1962), p. 142.

[191]*Ibid.*

[192]*Ibid.,* p. 141.

[193]Greeley, "The New Community," p. 34. This writer has a Discussion Club and a Prayer Group in St. Ursula's parish, Mount Vernon, N. Y. He meets with the former once a month and weekly with the latter. Every first Friday of the month he and the Prayer Group CELEBRATE the Eucharist together. It is always an indescribable event and a most genuine experience because it is the community's celebration with the full participation of all those present.

[194]*Blueprint for a Working Church.* A Study in New Pastoral Structures (St. Meinrad, Ind.: Abbey Press, 1973), p. 24. Cf. also J.-J. von Allmen's description of the four requirements of a place of worship: the Word of Christ proclaimed, the Lord's Supper celebrated, the minister recognized, and one's neighbor helped (*op. cit.,* p. 243).

[195]*Documents on Anglican-Roman Relations III* (Washington, D. C.: USCC Publications, 1976), p. 23.

[196]Bravo, *op. cit.,* p. 413.

[197]*Ibid.,* p. 436.

[198]*Ibid.,* pp. 438-439.

[199]It is interesting to note on this point that Richard Currier, to counter Marx's concept of "the world as in process of EVOLUTION, with man as its focal point," introduces the term INVOLUTION in reference to worship conceiving of "man and his world as being in a process of greater and greater involvement into the world of a higher Being. . . . This process of

involution in God's world is WORSHIP." *Restructuring the Parish* (Chicago, Illinois: Argus Press, Incorporated, 1967), pp. 27-28.

[200]J.-J. von Allmen, *op. cit.*, pp. 55-56. John J. Harmon also uses very powerful language in describing the effects of the Eucharist in an article, "The Parish: When Is It Alive?—When Should It Die?" *Cross Currents* (1965), p. 390: "When the Eucharist is done in a parish, the reality that should be signified is nothing less than a real presence of God on the streets surrounding the altar as on the altar itself. And the parish that resists its mission on the streets, to expose and implement this saving presence of God in the common life of believer and unbeliever, by this very fact will resist a full exposure of the presence of God within the Eucharist itself—no matter how explicit the ceremony, how attractive the preaching, how understandable the rite, and how edifying the architecture.

"Consider how the Emmaus story establishes this necessary interconnection between God's presence both in the meal and in the world within which the meal occurs. . . . First the meeting with Christ on the street, and the attempt to understand God's activity among men; then the meal itself, in which—very significantly—as soon as the disciples recognized him, he vanished; and finally their summation of the event: 'Did we not feel our hearts on fire *as he talked with us on the road* and explained the scriptures to us?' (Lk. 24:32; NEB). The point is very simple: the graceful exposure of Christ's presence is *necessarily* both in the meal and on the road; neither is complete without the other. *The Emmaus story directly contradicts our persistent over-objectification of Christ's presence in the sacraments, and our equally persistent under- or non-objectification of his presence in his world.*"

[201]"Creating A Community," James O'Gara (ed.), *The Postconciliar Parish*, p. 111.

[202]*Op. cit.*, p. 58.

[203]Decree on the Apostolate of the Laity (*AA*), no. 10; Abbott, *op. cit.*, p. 501.

[204]James D. Anderson, *To Come Alive*. New Proposal for Revitalizing the Local Church (New York: Harper & Row, Publishers, 1973), p. 11.

[205]Cf. *CD*, no. 27 and *AA*, no. 26; Abbott, *op. cit.*, pp. 416, 515.

[206]*Op. cit.*,p.X. He also adds:"The faithful assemble around the altar, but they cannot stop there. The role of the Christian community is to bear witness to God in the world, to bring God to the world and the world to God. Parishioners are neighbors, but this must mean more than neighbors in a narrow or territorial sense. The parish must not simply worship at the altar; it must embrace and ennoble all of human life. The Communion of the Saints cuts across continents and centuries; it joins black and white, rich and poor; it joins the Christian in America with the Christian in Africa or Asia; it joins the Christian of the twentieth century with Thomas Aquinas and Benedict Joseph Labre. It is toward this openness, this catholicity, that the parochial community must work. And in this connection I, as a layman, must note the difficulties under which we labor" (*ibid.*, pp. X-XI).

[207]Jasper J. Chiodini, "Vatican II in Suburbia," James O'Gara, *op. cit.*, p. 63.

[208]Cf. *ibid.*, pp. 65-79; Robert C. Broderick, *The Parish Council Handbook* and *Your Parish Comes Alive* (Chicago, Illinois: Franciscan Herald Press, 1968 and 1970); Bernard Lyons, *Parish Councils.* Renewing the Chris-

tian Community (Techny, Illinois; Divine Word Publications, 1967); David P. O'Neill, *The Sharing Community* (Dayton, Ohio: Pflaum Press, 1968); Stephen B. Clark, *Building Christian Communities* (Notre Dame, Indiana: Ave Maria Press, 1972); James D. Glasse, *Putting It Together in the Parish* (New York: Abingdon Press, 1972); Andrew M. Greeley, *The Church and the Suburbs* (New York: Sheed & Ward, 1959); Leo R. Ward, C.S.C., *The Living Parish* (Notre Dame, Indiana: Fides Publishers Association, 1959).

[209]*PO*, no. 6; Abbott, *op. cit.*, p. 544.

[210]Chiodini, *art cit.*, O'Gara, *op. cit.*, p. 65.

[211]David P. O'Neill, *The Sharing Community*, p. 23.

[212]*LG*, no. 30; Abbott, *op. cit.*, p. 57; the same document, no. 37, also instructs pastors to "encourage the layman so that he may undertake tasks on his own initiative" and propose projects, suggestions and desires. Furthermore, the hope is expressed that familiar dialogue will be created between the laity and their pastors and it will result in a strengthened sense of personal responsibility on the part of the laity (Abbott, *op. cit.*, p. 65). The Pastoral Constitution on the Church in the Modern World strikes a similar note by saying: "Furthermore, it is to be hoped that many laymen will receive an appropriate formation in the sacred sciences, and that some will develop and deepen these studies by their own labors. In order that such persons may fulfill their proper function, let it be recognized that all the faithful, clerical and lay, possess a lawful freedom of inquiry and of thought, and the freedom to express their minds humbly and courageously about those matters in which they enjoy competence" (Abbott, *op. cit.*, p. 270).

Joseph T. Nolan, recognizing the Council's expectations and the many obstacles to them on the parish level, sums up his experiences in the parish: "Apart from inadequate priestly training, probably the greatest obstacle to a genuine vitality in the parish *is a closed mind*. There is no desire to change, in Newman's sense: this is a condition of living here below, 'and to be perfect is to have changed often.' This state of the status quo shows up very much in dioceses where the Ordinary was unable to attend all the Council sessions because of age or illness. It was also possible to attend and still remain insulated from all the excitement of new ideas. In these dioceses they still issue directives forbidding home visits and imposing an 11 o'clock curfew; directives on liturgy are usually prohibitory; the advice on ecumenism is to go slow; opinions on social problems like fair housing and integration are non-existent" (O'Gara, *op. cit.*, p. 90).

[213]Greeley, "The Question of the Parish. . . ." p. 140.

[214]*Ibid.*, pp. 141-143.

[215]*AA*, no. 9; Abbott, *op. cit.*, p. 500.

[216]*LG*, no. 33, *AA*, no. 3; Abbott, *op. cit.*, pp. 59, 492.

[217]*AA*, no. 10; Abbott, *op. cit.*, p. 501.

[218]Cf. *ibid.*

[219]*Ibid.*, no. 14; Abbott, *op. cit.*, pp. 505-506.

[220]*Ibid.*, no. 27; Abbott, *op. cit.*, p. 516.

[221]Joseph Gremillion, "The Parish and the World We Live In," *The Parish In A Time of Change*, pp. 197-198.

[222]"Building Christian Community," *The Parish in a Time of Change*, p. 23.

[223]Richard Currier, *Restructuring the Parish*, p. 65; Currier even recom-

mends that a thorough study of the area be the first step toward promoting parish life. The whole area should be broken down into ten districts; a district into seven to ten sections; a section into ten grass-root territorial units. He also gives samples, and calls the neighborhood unit of ten families Neighborhood Communion signifying the sign-element of the parish.

224Winter, *op. cit.*, p. 34.

225*Ibid.*, p. 50. One of the committees that should be established as soon as the parish council is called into existence is the Public Affairs Committee. Unfortunately, there are very few parish councils in the United States that would consider such a committee a vital part of their operations. Though no statistical figures are available to this writer, it is certainly regrettable that parish councils have been thought of almost exclusively in parochial, ghetto-ish categories. Perhaps, this narrow-minded, self-centered attitude is the true cause of their ephemeral existence.

226St. Meinrad, Indiana: Abbey Press. In the same year it was previously published in Great Britain under the title *Mission or Maintenance* by Darton, Longman & Todd Limited. Although it is primarily the fruit of the English experience in regard to parish life, it has much to offer to the American readers. We will utilize, therefore, especially those ideas of the book that can be claimed as valid and representative of parish life here in the United States, too. The author deserves attention because, in addition to his pastoral work in Great Britain, he had also spent some of his seventeen years of pastoral ministry in Switzerland, Italy, and the United States.

227*Ibid.*, p. 1.

228*Ibid.*, p. 5.

229*Ibid.*, p. 7.

230*Ibid.*, p. 11.

231*Ibid.*, p. 23.

232*Ibid.*, p. 40.

233Cf. *Ibid.*

234*Ibid.*, p. 42.

235*Ibid.*, p. 61.

236*Ibid.*, pp. 62-63.

237*Ibid.*, p. 62.

238*Ibid.*, p. 118.

239Cf. *ibid.*

240*Ibid.*, p. 119.

241*Ibid.*, p. 120.

242*Ibid.*, p. 104.

243Dennis Clark, "Parochial Roles," John McCudden (ed.), *The Parish in Crisis* (Techny, Illinois: Divine Word Publications, 1967), p. 46. The call for structural changes has been heard in Protestant circles as well. Cf. Martin E. Marty, *Death and Birth of the Parish* (Saint Louis: Concordia, 1964). Even the title of the book indicates the demand for such changes.

244*Etudes de Sociologie Religieuse* (Paris, II, 1952).

245Floristan, *op. cit.*, p. 123.

246Joseph E. Ciesluk, *National Parishes in the United States.* The Catholic University of America Canon Law Studies No. 190 (Washington, D.C.: The Catholic University of America Press, 1944), p. 27. Unfortunately, even in later years, many Catholics lost their faith or at least their affiliation with their local community. It is edifying to note, however, that when Bishop John England set out to visit the priest-less laity scattered all over the three-state diocese of North Carolina, South Carolina, and Georgia in 1821, he found Catholics who had preserved the faith and handed it over to their children without any help from priests and without the presence of any form of ecclesiastical structures. Many times the bishop gave oral or written commission to a few of the more prominent members of these isolated Catholic communities to conduct what we call now paraliturgical services on Sundays and holidays and to teach catechism to children and others. It is only regrettable that these commissioned lay leaders very often failed in carrying out their sacred duties. Personal disputes and the lukewarm attitude of the people, even of converts, were to be blamed for it. Cf. "Diurnal of the Right Reverend John England, First Bishop of Charleston, South Carolina, 1820-1823," *Records of the American Historical Society*, vol. 6, pp. 37, 39, 198, etc.

I am grateful for the permission granted to me by Dr. Patrick Carey, a former student of mine and presently professor of Religious Studies at Carleton College, Northfield, Minnesota, to utilize in this part of the study the result of his research into the history of the Church in America.

247Cf. Fergus Macdonald, C.P., "The Development of Parishes in the United States," C. J. Nuesse and Thomas J. Harte, C.Ss.R. (eds.), *The Sociology of the Parish*. An Introductory Symposium (Milwaukee: The Bruce Publishing Co., 1951), pp. 45-71. See also Theodore Maynard, *The Story of American Catholicism* (New York: Macmillan Co., 1943); Gerald Shaughnessy, S.M., *Has the Immigrant Kept the Faith?* (New York: Macmillan Co., 1952). The 1833 pastoral letter of the entire American hierarchy is a good indication of the problems affecting the lives of the Catholic laity. They wrote in part: "We exhort those good persons to continue faithful. Let them fortify their faith, by reading those explanations and compilations which are calculated to strengthen themselves and to enable them to instruct their children; let them be earnest and regular in the great duty of prayer, especially on the Lord's day, the holy days and days of devotion; on these occasions, we advise them to assemble together if there be two or more families, and uniting in spirit with the priest who offers the holy sacrifice in their vicinity, or with the bishop of the Diocese, let them at the usual hour of worship unless some other be more convenient, recite their form of prayers for the Mass, read some approved books of instruction, or some Catholic sermon": *1833 Pastoral of the American Hierarchy*, Peter Guilday (ed.), *The National Pastorals of the American Hierarchy* (1792-1919) (Washington, D C.: National Catholic Welfare Council, 1923), p. 73.

248Cf., for example, Thomas T. McAvoy, *A History of the Catholic Church in the United States* (Notre Dame, Ind.: University of Notre Dame Press, 1969); John Gilmary Shea, *The History of the Catholic Church in the United States*, 4 vols. (New York: Harper & Bros., 1939), etc.

249America was a mission territory under the control and authority of the Congregation for the Propagation of the Faith up to June 29, 1908 in spite of the fact that actually the missionary activity meant care-taking of believers and not converting unbelievers. History has passed a severe judgment on one of the most colorful and activist Catholic layman of the entire history of the Catholic Church in America, Dr. John F. Oliveira Fernandez, a lay Trustee of the Norfolk, Virginia, parish. Though his sources and background as well as his exaggerations in regard to ecclesial structures easily provoked a negative reaction and judgment, it is recognized today that it was Dr. Fernandez who had a clear vision of the new opportunities available to the local communities and to the universal Church in America. Cf. Letter J. Fernandez to Messrs. Donoghy and Moran, May 31, 1817, P. Guilday, *The Catholic Church in Virginia (1815-1822).* Series VIII. United States Catholic Historical Society Monograph (New York: The United States Catholic Historical Society, 1924). Though Dr. Fernandez' views were extreme, it must have been a refreshing experience to find a layman with real theological interest and background. For the general situation points to a rather "parochial" mentality as prevalent in the United States with cultural and ethnic ghettos, consciously isolated from the wider community. This remark should not be interpreted in the negative, however. For the national and ethnic parishes actually provided to the immigrants the intermediate milieu for assimilation into the Catholic life of America. For details, cf. Thomas J. Harte, C.Ss.R., "Racial and National Parishes in the United States," Nuesse and Harte, *op. cit.*, pp. 154-177; see also Ciesluk, *op. cit.*, p. 53. For the "parochial" mentality, the "Instruction to the Bishops of the United States Concerning Public Schools" of the Congregation for the Propaganda of the Faith, 1875, is significant in its declaration that it was against both the natural law and the divine law for Catholic students to attend non-Catholic schools. Cf. James Michael Lee, "The Parish and the Catholic School," M. Bordelon (ed.), *The Parish in a Time of Change*, p. 44.

250It is unfortunate, but again only natural, that the experience of the new freedom, independence, and financial support voluntarily given to the parish, led them to the hope of not only helping but also controlling their local religious community and using it for their own personal gain, prestige or hunger for power. Fernandez' views represent, in many respects, such aberrations. He not only advocated a managerial role of the temporal affairs for the lay Trustees but also the power of hiring and firing local parish employees, choosing a qualified pastor, superintending his moral and professional life and, in cases of unbecoming or scandalous personal conduct, firing him with the approval of the majority of the congregation. Furthermore, he claimed very far reaching roles for the laity in running the entire diocese through electing the bishop and forming, on an equal basis with the pastors, the "Supreme Ecclesiastical Synodus" that would actually have decided the policies of the diocese. Cf. Letter J. Fernandez to Messrs. Donoghy and Moran, P. Guilday, *op. cit.*, pp. 55-56. Dr. Fernandez' theological sources are good indications of the direction of his ideological orientation: Nicholas of Cusa, Jean Gerson, Johann Mosheim, and Justinus Febronius.

251This claim of Dr. Fernandez rests on his understanding of the Church as the great association and union of Christians. In no circumstances should it ever be identified with the hierarchy. Though laity and clergy have different functions in the union, they share equally in the responsibilities of the parish communities.

252*The Works of the Right Reverend John England*, collected and arranged by the Right Reverend I. A. Reynolds (Baltimore: John Murphy & Co., 1849), vol. V, pp. 91-110. England was not entirely positive or uncritical on trusteeism and the whole complex issue of lay involvement in church affairs. He called, for example, some Trustees "Catholic Atheists." This term in itself is already a reflection on those who tried to exploit the issue for their own selfish purposes. Furthermore, England was very critical of ". . . the ridiculous and mischievous efforts of some misguided men in this country, who know very little about their religion, and never practice its duties, to constitute themselves as a new kind of governors, under the name of vestries and Patrons" (Reynolds, *op. cit.*, I, p. 332). England did not even hesitate to spell out some similarities between the abuses created by the Trustee-system in America and the abuses of the Lay Investiture promoted in Medieval Europe. Cf. *ibid.*, pp. 242, 332, 461, etc.

[253]Ciesluk, *op. cit.*, p. 46.

[254]The Constitution organized the diocese into a number of parish churches. Each church was to create its own elected vestry. It was composed of the priest and a group of elected lay representatives. Managing of the temporalities of the parish belonged to the vestry. Furthermore, each vestry would send its priest and an elected lay representative to a yearly convention of the entire diocese. The convention was made up of a house of the laity and a house of the clergy, with the bishop presiding. Their primary competence was ecclesiastical temporalities though the delegates could discuss matters of a spiritual nature as well. Decisions were reached by voting on diocesan matters. It must be admitted that this democratic approach to church government clearly acknowledged the communal nature of the Church. It also provided a learning experience for both clergy and laity.

[255]It is possible that this trend established so early in the history of the Church in America has been responsible for the lack of structural innovation as well as for the total absence of a genuinely American theology. Somehow the human condition as it has been experienced in this country was not allowed to ferment theological and ecclesial thinking.

[256]We must emphasize, however, that there have also been some positive moments in this respect in the history of the American Church. One such moment is represented by the life of Isaac Hecker (1819-1888), founder of the Paulist Fathers. This "modern Paul," as he has been called, was a man of the people and from the people who worked unstintingly to recommend the Catholic Faith to the democratic American people. He was an ardent American, deeply appreciative of American institutions but likewise absolutely and uncompromisingly Catholic. He thus attempted to take hold of the golden opportunity offered him by the situation of the Church in the New World. And he succeeded so admirably that his name came wrongly to be associated with a-movement to go too far in one direction which received the name of "Americanism."

[257]"Two American Views of the Laity: 1800-1842," an unpublished paper. Joseph N. Moody has made very pertinent observations in regard to the same point in his article, "Permanence and Flexibility in Parish Life," M. Bordelon (ed.), *The Parish in a Time of Change*. First, in dealing with the perennial temptation of Christian life, he writes: "This description of the Church as the Israel of the New Exodus which the early Fathers used so frequently has a practical conclusion. The basic temptation of the old Israel in the desert was the desire to settle down, to find a spot with shade and water, to make itself comfortable, and to resist the will of God to move forward toward its goal. Movement involves effort, and we are inclined to avoid it. We generally prefer to remain in familiar surroundings rather than

to venture into the unknown" (p. 2). Then, explicitly referring to the American past, he says that in spite of many deficiencies, "in the first stage of our national history, American Catholicism had already received its fundamental character: it was constructively orientated toward American institutions, and it conceived its future in terms of an adaptation to American culture" (*ibid.*, p. 12). Because of this orientation the American parish had the unique heritage of facilitating the social integration of its people without losing the lowly. At the same time, the parish system failed in a disturbing measure to serve adequately its "greatest challenge and brightest hope," the growing community of American Catholic intellectuals (cf. *ibid.*, pp. 13-15). We are still suffering from this failure today. For "common sense ministry" without theological vision and contemporary alertness is acceptable to those only who do not intend any challenge to the ministers of God.

In the present system of selecting or appointing pastors to different parishes the main criterion is the year of ordination, i.e., seniority. Even today there are not enough instances in which creativity and personal responsibility of younger priests would be systematically developed, tried and tested. Though many times intellectually better prepared than their elders, these younger priests have to wait for the time of fading curiosity and failing health to try new ways and new methods for the people of God.

[258]Daniel Morrisey, O.P., "Preface," Karl Rahner, *Theology of Pastoral Action,* p. 16.

[255]Dennis Clark, "Parochial Roles," John McCudden (ed.), *The Parish in Crisis,* p. 46. Cf. also Francis B. Donnelly, "The Pastoral Ministry in Transition," Nuesse and Harte, *The Sociology of the Parish,* pp. 285-302.

[260]Foster, *Requiem for a Parish,* p. 98.

[261]*Ibid.*, p. 106.

[262]Cf. "American Catholicism: toward the year 2000," *Theology Digest,* 20 (1972), pp. 341-348; cf. also Raymond Lemieux, "The Church and the Survival of Canada," *The Ecumenist,* 11 (1973), pp. 56-60. The following passage is greatly relevant to the center point of this study: "The Church, herself a collectivity, cannot remain indifferent to any value actually experienced by men. Her rootedness in a Gospel that claims to transcend the conditions of history forces her to relate herself to all other transcendent values men have experienced and to their ethics and politics. As a collectivity, her role is to approve or to contest the objectives men set up to ensure their betterment. She must, therefore, clarify her order of values so as to be able to relate to her own value system the value of the survival of Canada or of national reconciliation presented in the life of society" (p. 56). The article even brings revelation and the human condition together as it singles out the local church as a locus of religious experience: "Through this religious experience a human group, reaching beyond the juridical membership of the institution, lays hold of universal vision made absolute and sacred, beyond all doubt. It formulates here what I will call the limit understanding of its human experience, the border line between what it can conceive of, explain and control and that other reality which it names Otherness. The Churches are then the privileged locus through which such sociologically constituted groups structure their personality and find in the absolute their action in the course of human affairs" (p. 58). Cf. also Thomas McGowan, "American Theology," *Commonweal,* 30 June, 1972, pp. 353-356; Herbert

W. Richardson, *Toward an American Theology* (New York: Harper & Row, 1967).

[263]Cf. Sullivan, *ibid.*, pp. 341-342. Though Sullivan readily admits that such democratic development will not affect the "given," the revelation of Christ which he considers as "the ontic and noetic *a priori* of Catholicism," he strongly adheres to the conviction that in its operational apparatus the Church must embrace a democratic mode "if she is to be part of the life of the twentieth century, if she is to preach the gospel today rather than yesterday" (p. 343).

[264]*Ibid.*, pp. 344-345.

[265]*Ibid.*, p. 346. We might also recall that it was the American emphasis on freedom that gave rise to John Courtney Murray, S.J., who was greatly responsible for promoting personal religious freedom here in the United States in his writings and lectures and was the chief architect of the Vatican II Declaration on Religious Freedom.

[266]*Ibid.* Sullivan finds this "drive and demand" as a reaction to two features of American life: privatization and "mass-ism." The first, manifesting itself in "the separation and introversion of the life of the individual," provokes personalism that is social. The second, by negative reaction, is counterbalanced by a community, by "a group where the personal and interpersonal are dominant." The following passage reflects the struggle as one faces the future: "This search for community is symbolized so attractively and powerfully in the zany lyricism of *Alice's Restaurant*. The movement of this film comes from the hope that you will be able to find 'anything you want.' And it is clear that 'what you want' is a community, a sense of belonging, a place where people care. The search for acceptance, understanding, for community, goes on all about us. It expresses itself in the hippie communes of the valleys of California and in the community houses of university towns. It moves Christians toward the formation of interest communities and floating parishes. It is—although largely unrecognized in this form—the force driving many religious communities to greater efforts at reform and renewal. The great symbol of the search is Woodstock and its goal, a Woodstock that will be more than a weekend. How ironic it is, how tragic, and yet how germane to the discussion of the future of Catholicism that the search for the new community in *Alice's Restaurant* takes place in a deconsecrated church!" (p. 347).

[267]*Ibid.*, p. 348. Cf. Thomas F. O'Meara and Donald M. Weisser, *Projections: Shaping an American Theology for the Future* (Garden City, N. Y.: Doubleday & Co., 1970), pp. 1-17.

[268]*Projections*, p. 4.

[269]Cf. chapter II of this book for the human condition and the teaching of Vatican II.

[270]Thomas McGowan, "American Theology," *Commonweal*, June, 30, 1972, p. 353. The contemporary relevance of the problem is very important. "The pattern of the rural parish in 18th century America, to be sure, was itself an adaptation. It was not the pattern of 12th century Italy or 1st century Palestine. It had made its necessary adjustments to the requirements of its time and place. Thus if we refuse to make some accommodation to the urbanization, population changes, new conditions of work and leisure, health and family living, racial and other conflicts that characterize our time, we

are not adhering to a tradition that has always existed apart from the culture of earlier periods. We are only stubbornly insisting on continuing an accommodation to a former, agrarian world which now no longer exists" (*Ministry for Tomorrow*. Report of the Special Committee on Theological Education. Nathan M. Pusey, Chairman, Charles L. Taylor, Director of Study; New York: The Seabury Press, 1967, p. 4). The reader should remember that the above text was written with Protestant parishes in mind. It is only partially applicable to Roman Catholic parishes in the United States. As a matter of fact, because of Catholic dependence on Europe for both theology and leadership, Catholic theology could never develop specifically American insights into the meaning of Christianity in the same way as Protestant theology has done. Even the article quoted above is more a tribute to Protestant than Roman Catholic thought and effort. However, theological and structural accommodation is a necessity in this country to create new openness to truth coming to us in dialogue with the human condition and with all kinds of different people. In dialogue one reads and listens, and observes *to learn* from others, not just *to evaluate* them in the conviction that one has inherited the whole truth and there was nothing that one could learn from others. Cf. Gregory Baum, "Tension in the Catholic Church," *The Ecumenist*, 7 (1969), pp. 21-26.

271John Ramon Mason, "Toward an American Theology: An Appraisal," *The Ecumenist*, 7 (1969), p. 27.

272Cf. Patrick Granfield, *Ecclesial Cybernetics: A Study of Democracy in the Church* (New York: The Macmillan Co., 1973). On pages 19-125, Granfield develops four examples of cybernetic analysis from the history of the Church: the slavery question, the birth control debate, the ecumenical movement, and the priestly celibacy controversy. The same procedure could be applied to the life of the American parish. It is also comforting to know that more than a quarter of a century ago it was already proposed that the entire pastoral ministry be recast in harmony with the demands of direct and personal contact, and of the environmental factors that shape individuals and parish communities. One can see a clear reference in the demand to input and feedback. Cf. Francis B. Donnelly, "The Pastoral Ministry in Transition," C. J. Nuesse and Thomas J. Harte, C.Ss.R. (eds.), *The Sociology of the Parish* (Milwaukee: The Bruce Publishing Co., 1950), p. 292.

273*Ministry for Tomorrow*, p. 21; cf. also *ibid.*, p. 7.

274"Evangelism in the Neo-Pagan Situation," *Mission Trends No. 2*, edited by Gerald H. Anderson and Thomas F. Stransky, C.S.P. (New York: Paulist Press and Grand Rapids: Wm. B. Eerdmans Publishing Co., 1975), p. 125. Cf. also Fred Smith, M.M., "The Mutuality of Evangelization: Father Inocente Salazar," *ibid.*, pp. 139-144. Pages 143-144 are exceptionally significant for reaffirming the validity of the human condition. One of Salazar's principles called for the realization "that as the missionary does not have all the answers, it is a two-way street between him and the people. There is a mutual revealing of God between them that ultimately enriches and helps each to become fully himself." In statements like this, one can see the verification of Cardinal Mercier's claim that "after the Bible, the most important and most instructive subject for study that the representative of Christ on earth can have is society" (Letter from Cardinal Mercier to Cardinal Gibbons, Sept. 25, 1921, *Oeuvres pastorales,* VIII, 259, quoted by Floristan, *op. cit.,* p. 29). And Floristan adds his remark that it is impossible to distinguish the religious and social aspects of human life in many religions. "Jesus Christ is the one who drew a line of differentiation, though not of absolute separation" (*ibid.,* p. 130).

[275]"Failure in Faith: Failure in Preaching," *America,* August 19, 1972, pp. 94-96.

[276]*Ibid.*

[277]*Ibid.,* p. 95. It is not this writer's duty or even aspiration to spell out concrete pastoral details in regard to homilies, but he cannot resist asking the question: Could anyone ever claim in good conscience that he is delivering the Word of God today in his homily read from a collection of sermons compiled sixty or seventy years ago? Such delivery is as tragic as reading notes to a sociology class prepared forty years ago. Or could a pastor be so preoccupied with his financial drive that he completely overlooks the Word of God in his homily on Pentecost Sunday?

[278]May, *ibid.,* p. 95. Very appropriately, he calls attention to the new trend of "peer evaluation"; he also advocates rigorous examination of preaching competence by the listeners. Some structural help in this direction would certainly introduce a more critical approach to preaching.

[279]Cf. Decree on the Bishops' Pastoral Office in the Church, no. 30; Abbott, *op. cit.,* p. 418; Decree on the Missionary Activity of the Church, no. 6; Abbott, *op. cit.,* p. 591, etc.

[280]"Celebrating Change: Communications and Theology," *Projections,* p. 167. What he says about theologians is also applicable to the preachers of the Word of God. Yes, European influence, the traditional priest-oriented attitude has prevailed too long in this country. Because changes in communications are usually irreversible processes, "they involve both theologian and audience in radically different orientations. Even if we can expect Europe to pursue the directions already in progress in America, we cannot look for leadership to a culture just entering the communications age" (*ibid.*)

[281]*Ibid.,* p. 169.

[282]Eucharistic celebrations for children, teenagers, students, nursing homes, hospitals, etc. should be handled as carefully planned salutary means of salvation, and not as luxuries available only on an irregular basis. To ignore the problem as nonexistent or to write off any segment of the parish community as an impossible task is only a recognition of the minister's inability to deal with today's problems and requirements. On the other hand, it must also be clearly stated here that, unfortunately, history has somehow lost its meaning and regulatory role for many of our contemporaries. This fact alone makes the minister's work extremely precarious. As Charles R. Feilding puts it: "The Churches can no longer take for granted a respectful hearing for anything whatever in their traditions" (*Education for Ministry.* Dayton, Ohio: American Association of Theological Schools, 1966, p. 5).

[283]"A Glimpse of Tomorrow's Church," *Cross Currents,* Spring, 1973, p. 22.

[284]*Ibid.* p. 23. The text is evidently a reference to the persecutions of the Church behind the Iron and Bamboo Curtains, but in its general tone

it is certainly applicable to the minority status of the Church almost in any country. Furthermore, it stresses the need for a more thorough preparation of those who will devote themselves to the service of God's people. The time has passed when one could claim that ordination to the priesthood automatically qualifies an individual to deal with issues and answers. The part-time ministers would bring experience and new talent to ministry. And the fact that they would continue their own profession would certainly prevent them from becoming mere functionaries in the community. They would operate as priests of their unit or units, and together with other priests, deacons, and priest-president or coordinator they would form the entire parish-team of ministers. The fact that no mention is made here of women ministers should not be interpreted as a negative judgment on the issue, only as an effort not to cloud the main issue by raising tempers.

285This is not a rejection of older pastors but merely a call for continual updating, learning, modernity, and flexibility. And most of all, it calls for the great gift and virtue of listening ability. The Holy Spirit speaks to us, in most cases, through the experiences and understanding of others. A rectory without consultation, a parish without dialogue might be an excellent place for the complacent and routine ministers. It cannot, however, be a place where the Word of God acts as a generating and revealing agent. The whole issue is not necessarily a question of age. A person can be intellectually old or even dead at twenty-five while a young-in-spirit John XXIII can put all of us to shame with his ever receptive mind.

The new attitude is suggested by a comparison between what has been and what should be the role—or between the passive stance and the active stance—of the minister of the local community. "A *passive stance* in relation to change produces adaptation. An *active stance* produces innovation. The passive pastor will be a *problem-solver*, dealing with those problems and issues that are thrust upon him. He will do what he has to do, when he has to do it, trying always to adapt to the changes so that he is not defeated or destroyed by them. This style might have been effective in a time of slower, simpler change. But it will not do today. The active pastor will become a problem-seeker, a pioneer moving toward problems not yet perceived by others, not yet popular in the culture": James D. Glasse, *Putting It Together in the Parish* (New York: Abington Press, 1972), p. 18. It is impossible to evaluate students of Catholic seminaries from the viewpoint of psychological makeup. But if they fall in line with their counterparts in Protestant seminaries, the picture is far from encouraging. James D. Glasse describes the Protestant seminarians thus: "We attract a rather high percentage of passive-dependent and passive-aggressive students to seminaries. If we do not have a better model for the ministry than this matched pair of caricatures we can do very little to help seminarians learn how to change themselves, their work, or the church, let alone the community" (*Ibid.*, p. 21).

286Cf. Glasse, *ibid.*, p. 139.

287Saint Louis: Concordia, 1964, pp. v & 4. Marty affirms clearly that to bring about the birth of the parish successfully, patient attention to detail is absolutely necessary.

288Cf. S.J. Kilian, O.F.M., "The Mission of the Church: To Divinize or To Humanize? A Response," *Proceedings of the Catholic Theological*

Society of America, 1976.

[289]S.J. Kilian, O.F.M., "Fundamental Option, An Essential Datum of the Human Person," *The American Benedictine Review,* 21 (1970), pp. 198-199. The article gives a fuller, more detailed picture of the entire problem.

[290]Cf., for example, V.J. Pospishil, *Divorce and Remarriage: Towards a New Catholic Teaching* (New York: Herder and Herder, 1967) and the *Commonweal* issue on "Divorce" (April 14, 1967).

[291]Kilian, "Fundamental Option . . . ," p. 199.

[292]S.J. Kilian, O.F.M., "The Question of Authority in 'Humanae Vitae,'" *Thought,* 44 (1969), p. 339 and "Authority in the Church," *ibid.,* pp. 69-82.

[293]John J. Harmon, "Parochial Imbalance and Fraternal Solidarity," John McCudden (ed.), *The Parish in Crisis,* p. 4. He claims that in this sense baptism is not only the incorporation into the body of Christ in separation from the human whole but a conscious reaffirmation also of the previous incorporation into the body of mankind. Cf. *ibid.,* p. 18.

[294]"Whether the Church continues in its pursuit of holiness without deep involvement in the world's problems—content, in the words of the Japanese theologian, merely to fish people out of the 'dirty river called the world'—or whether it plunges into full participation in an effort to help clean up the river itself, one thing is certain: it must have a clear understanding of the dominant physical and social features of this turbulent stream of modern life. Whether we like it or not, the character of the Church's membership, its preaching, its program, its finances, its very location, to say nothing of myriad individual demands upon its ministry, are crucially affected by several key factors which we call 'secular'" (*Ministry for Tomorrow,* p. 13).

[295]"Toward an American Theology: An Appraisal," *The Ecumenist,* 7 (1969), p. 26.

[296]*Toward an American Theology* (New York: Harper & Row, 1967), p. 44.

BIBLIOGRAPHY

For a more complete bibliography the reader should consult Casiano Floristan, *The Parish—Eucharistic Community* and Alex Blöchlinger, *The Modern Parish Community* (both fully cited below). The following bibliography has been restricted to mostly English works, but foreign titles have been included where important.

BOOKS

Abbott, Walter M., S.J., ed., *The Documents of Vatican II*, New York, The America Press, 1966.

Alves, Rubem A., *A Theology of Human Hope*, St. Meinrad, Indiana, Abbey Press, 1972.

Amalorpavadass, D.S., *Approach, Meaning and Horizon of Evangelization*, Bangalore, National Biblical, Catechetical and Liturgical Center, 1973.

Anderson, Gerald H. and Stransky, Thomas F., C.S.P., eds., *Mission Trends*, Numbers 1 and 2, New York, Paulist Press, and Grand Rapids, Wm. B. Eerdmans Pub. Co., 1974.

Anderson, James D., *To Come Alive! New Proposal for Revitalizing the Local Church*, New York, Harper & Row, Publishers, 1973.

Biersdorf, John E., *Hunger for Experience, Vital Religious*

Communities in America, New York, Seabury Press, 1975.

Blöchlinger, Alex., *The Modern Parish Community.* Translated by Geoffrey Stevens, New York, P.J. Kenedy & Sons, 1965.

Bordelon, Marvin, ed., *The Parish in a Time of Change,* Notre Dame, Fides Publishers, Inc., 1967.

Bouscaren, T. Lincoln, S.J. and Ellis, Adam C., S.J., *Canon Law, A Text and Commentary,* Milwaukee, The Bruce Pub. Co., 1949.

Bravo, Francisco, *The Parish of San Miguelito in Panama,* Cuernavaca, Mexico, Sondeos, 1966.

Broderick, Robert C., M.A., *The Parish Council Handbook, A Handbook to Bring the Power of Renewal to Your Parish,* Chicago, Franciscan Herald Press, 1968.

—————-., *Your Parish Comes Alive,* Chicago, Franciscan Herald Press, 1970.

Brown, Robert McAfee, *Frontiers for the Church Today,* New York, Oxford University Press, 1973.

Ciesluk, Joseph E., J.C.L., *National Parishes in the United States,* No. 190 in The Catholic University of America *Canon Law Studies,* Washington, D.C., The Catholic University of America Press, 1944.

Clark, Stephen B., *Building Christian Communities, Strategy for Renewing the Church,* Notre Dame, Ave Maria Press, 1972.

Combaluzier, Charles, *God Tomorrow.* Translated by Matthew J. O'Connell, New York, Paulist Press, 1972.

Colonnese, Louis Michael, ed., *The Church in the Present-Day Transformation of Latin America in the Light of the Council,* Second General Conference of Latin American Bishops, Bogota and Medellin, 1968, Bogota, Columbia, General Secretariat of *Celam,* 1970.

Congar, Yves, O.P., *A Gospel Priesthood,* New York, Herder & Herder, 1967.

—————-., *Vrai et fousse réforme dans l'Eglise,* Paris, du Cerf, 1952.

Curran, Charles E., and Hunt, Robert E., *Dissent In and For the Church, Theologians and Humanae Vitae*, New York, Sheed & Ward, Inc., 1969.

Curran, Charles E. and Dyer, George J., *Shared Responsibility in the Local Church*, A Project of the Catholic Theological Society of America, sponsored by the National Federation of Priests' Councils in conjunction with *Chicago Studies*, 1970.

Currier, Richard, *Restructuring the Parish*, Chicago, Argus Press, 1967.

de la Tour, G. Imbart, *Les paroisses rurales du IV^{ie} au XI^{ie} siècle*, Paris, 1900.

Delespesse, Max., *The Church Community, Leaven and Life Style*, Indiana, Ave Maria Press, 1968.

de Lubac, Henri, *Les Eglises particulières dans l'Eglise universelle*, Paris, Editions Aubier-Montaigne, 1971.

Diekmann, Godfrey, O.S.B., *Come, Let Us Worship*, Baltimore, Helicon Press, Inc., 1961.

Dulles, Avery, S.J., *Models of the Church*, Garden City, N.Y., Doubleday & Co., Inc., 1974.

Fecher, Charles A., *Parish Council Committee Guide*, Washington, D.C., National Council of Catholic Men, 1970.

Flanagan, Donal, ed., *The Meaning of the Church*, Dublin, Ireland, 1966.

Floristan, Casiani, *The Parish—Eucharistic Community*, translated by John F. Byrne, Notre Dame, Fides Publishers, Inc., 1964.

Foster, John, *Requiem For a Parish*, Westminster, Maryland, The Newman Press, 1962.

Gilkey, Langdon, *How the Church Can Minister to the World Without Losing Itself*, New York, Harper & Row, Publishers, 1964.

Glasse, James D., *Putting It Together in the Parish*, Nashville, Abingdon Press, 1972.

Godin, H. and Daniel, Y., *La France, pays de mission?*, Paris, Editeurs du Cerf, 1943.

Granfield, Patrick, *Ecclesial Cybernetics*, New York, The Macmillan Co., 1973.

Grasso, Domenico, *Proclaiming God's Message*, Notre Dame, 1965.

Gratsch, Edward J., *Where Peter Is, A Survey of Ecclesiology*, New York, Alba House, 1975.

Greeley, Andrew M., *The Church and the Suburbs*, New York, Sheed & Ward, 1959.

—————., *The Hesitant Pilgrim*, New York, Sheed & Ward, 1966.

Grichting, Wolfgang L., *Parish Structure and Climate In an Era of Change, A Sociologist's Inquiry*, Washington, D.C., Center for Applied Research in the Apostolate, 1969.

Guidelines For Parish Councils, New York, Archdiocese of New York, Commission on Parish Councils.

Guilday, P., *A History of the Councils of Baltimore*, New York, Macmillan Co., 1932.

—————., *The Catholic Church in Virginia* (1815-1822). Series VIII. New York, The United States Catholic Historical Society, 1924.

—————., *The National Pastorals of the American Hierarchy*, (1792-1919), Washington, D.C., National Catholic Welfare Council, 1923.

Hamer, Jerome, O.P., *The Church is a Communion.* Translated by Geoffrey Chapman, Ltd., (Ronald Matthews), New York, Sheed & Ward, 1964.

Haughton, Rosemary, *The Theology of Experience*, Paramus, New Jersey, The Newman Press, 1972.

Heilbrauer, Robert L., "The Impact of Technology, The Historic Debate" in Dunlop, John T., ed., *Automation and Technological Change*, Englewood Cliffs, Prentice-Hall, Inc., 1962.

Hillman, Eugene, *The Church as Mission*, New York, Herder & Herder, 1965.

Hinnebusch, Paul, O.P., *Community in the Lord*, Notre Dame, Ave Maria Press, 1975.

Holmes, Urban T. III, *The Future Shape of Ministry*, New York, Seabury Press, 1970.

Houtart, Fr., *The Church and the City Life*, Chicago, 1953.

Huxley, Julian, *Religion Without Revelation*, New York, The New American Library (Mentor Books), 1957.

Johnson, Robert Clyde, ed., *The Church and Its Changing Ministry*, Philadelphia, The General Assembly of the United Presbyterian Church, 1961.

Jozefzyk, A., *A Modern Parish as Modelled on the Life of the Cenacle*, Ph.D., dissertation, Angelicum, Rome, Fribourg, 1951.

Kloppenburg, Bonaventure, O.F.M., *The Ecclesiology of Vatican II*, translated by Matthew J. O'Connell, Chicago, Franciscan Herald Press, 1974.

Latourelle, René, S.J., *Theology: Science of Salvation*, translated by Sister Mary Dominic, New York, Alba House, 1969.

Luzbetak, Louis J., S.U.D., *The Church in the Changing City*, Techny, Ill., Divine Word Publications, 1966.

Lyons, Bernard, *Parish Councils: Renewing the Christian Community*, Foreword by Bishop John J. Wright, Techny, Ill, Divine Word Publications, 1967.

Macquarrie, John, *Twentieth Century Religious Thought, The Frontiers of Philosophy and Theology*, 1900-1960, New York, Harper & Row, 1963.

Marty, Martin E., ed., with Biegner, Paul R., Blumhorst, Roy and Young, Kenneth R., *Death and Birth of the Parish*, St. Louis, Concordia Publishing House, 1964.

Marty, Martin E., and Peerman, Dean G., eds., *New Theology Series*, nos. 1-6, 8, 10, New York, The Macmillan Co., 1964.

Marty, Martin E., *The Fire We Can Light, The Role of Religion in a Suddenly Different World*, Garden City, N. Y., Doubleday & Co., Inc., 1963.

Mathis, Marcian J., O.F.M., and Meyer, Nicholas W., O.F.M., eds., *The Pastoral Companion, A Handbook of Canon*

Law, 12th edition, Chicago, Franciscan Herald Press, 1961.

McCudden, John, ed., *The Parish in Crisis,* Techny, Ill., Divine Word Publications, 1967.

McGovern, James O., *The Church in the Churches,* Foreword by Jaroslav Pelikan, Washington, D.C., Corpus Books, 1968.

Meyendorff, John, *Orthodoxy and Catholicity,* New York, Sheed & Ward, Inc., 1966.

Michonneau, Abbé Georges, *My Father's Business: A Priest in France,* translated by Edmund Gilpin, New York, Herder & Herder, 1959.

————————., *Revolution in a City Parish.* Foreword by Archbishop Cushing, Westminster, Maryland, The Newman Press, 1949.

Mickells, A.A., *The Constitutive Elements in Parishes,* Washington, 1960.

Moehler, Johann A., *Symbolism or Exposition of the Doctrinal Differences Between Catholics and Protestants as Evidenced by Their Symbolic Writings.* Translated by James B. Robertson, 5th edition, London, Gibbings & Co., 1906.

Morris, Philip D., ed., *Metropolis: Christian Presence and Responsibility,* Notre Dame, Fides Publishers, Inc., 1970.

Motte, Jean-François, O.F.M., and Dourmap, Medard, O.F.M. Cap., *The New Parish Mission: The Work of the Church,* translated by Paul J. Oligny, O.F.M., Chicago, Franciscan Herald Press, 1962.

Neill, Stephen Charles and Weber, Hans-Ruedi, eds., *The Layman in Christian History,* A Project of the Department on the Laity of the World Council of Churches, Philadelphia, The Westminster Press, 1963.

Nicodemus, Donald E., *The Democratic Church,* Introduction by Gregory Baum, O.S.A., Milwaukee, The Bruce Pub. Co., 1969.

Nuesse, C.J. and Harte, Thomas J., C.Ss.R., eds., *The Sociol-*

ogy of the Parish, Milwaukee, The Bruce Pub. Co., 1951.

O'Dea, Thomas F., *The Catholic Crisis*, Boston, Beacon Press, 1968.

O'Donoghue, Joseph, *Elections in the Church*, Baltimore, Helicon Press, 1967.

O'Gara, James, ed., *The Postconciliar Parish*, Afterword by Archbishop Paul J. Hallinan, New York, P.J. Kenedy & Sons, 1967.

Oglesby, William B., Jr., ed., *The New Shape of Pastoral Theology*, Nashville, Abingdon Press, 1969.

Ohlig, Karl-Heinz, *Why We Need the Pope: The Necessity and Limits of Papal Primacy*. Translated by Dr. Robert C. Ware, St. Meinrad, Indiana, Abbey Press, 1975.

O'Meara, Thomas F. and Weisser, Donald M., *Projections: Shaping an American Theology for the Future*, Garden City, N.Y. Doubleday & Co., Inc., 1970.

O'Neill, David P., *The Sharing Community: Parish Councils and Their Meaning*, Dayton, Pflaum Press, 1968.

Power, John, *Mission Theology Today*, Maryknoll, New York, Orbis Books, 1971.

Powers, Joseph M., S.J., *Eucharistic Theology*, New York, Herder & Herder, 1967.

Proceedings, Bergamo Conference, pp. 15-17, *Diocesan Pastoral Council*, Washington, D.C., National Council of Catholic Men, 1970.

Pusey, Nathan M. and Taylor, Charles L., *Ministry for Tomorrow: Report of the Special Committee on Theological Education*, (Study sponsored by the Episcopal Church Foundation), New York, The Seabury Press, 1967.

Quinn, Bernard, *Toward a Job Description for the Non-Metropolitan Catholic Parish*, Washington, D.C., Center for Applied Research in the Apostolate, 1969.

Rahner, Hugh, S.J., ed., *The Parish from Theology to Practice*, translated by Robert Kress, Westminster, Maryland, The Newman Press, 1958.

Rahner, Karl, S.J., *Faith Today*, translated by Ray and Rosaleen Ockenden, London, Sheed & Ward, Ltd., 1967.

————————., *Nature and Grace, Dilemmas in the Modern Church*, New York, Sheed & Ward, 1964.

————————., with Ernst, Cornelius, O.P., and Smyth, Kevin, eds., *Sacramentum Mundi, An Encyclopedia of Theology*, 4 vols., New York, Herder & Herder, 1969.

————————., *The Christian Commitment: Essays in Pastoral Theology*. Translated by Cecily Hastings, New York, Sheed & Ward, Ltd., 1963.

————————., *The Christian of the Future*, translated by W.J. O'Hara, New York, Herder & Herder, 1967.

————————., *The Dynamic Element in the Church*, New York, Herder & Herder, 1964.

————————., *The Christian in the Market Place*, New York, Sheed & Ward, 1966.

————————., *Theological Investigations*, translated by Karl -H. Kruger, Vol. II, Baltimore, Helicon Press, London, Darton, Longman & Todd, Ltd., 1963, Vol. X, translated by David Bourke, New York, Herder & Herder, 1973.

————————., *The Shape of the Church to Come*, New York, Seabury Press, 1972.

————————., *Theology for Renewal: Bishops, Priests, Laity*, translated by Cecily Hastings and Richard Strachan, New York, Sheed & Ward, Ltd., 1964.

————————., and Daniel Morrissey, O.P., eds., *Theology of Pastoral Action*, Vol. 1, *Studies in Pastoral Theology*, New York, Herder & Herder, 1968.

Reynolds, I.A., *The Works of the Right Reverend John England*, Baltimore, John Murphy and Co., 1849.

Richardson, Herbert W., *Toward an American Theology*, New York, Harper & Row, 1967.

Robinson, John A.T., *Honest to God*, Philadelphia, The Westminster Press, 1963.

Schillebeeckx, E., *Church and World*, New York, Sheed & Ward, 1971.

Schlink, Edmund, *The Coming Christ and the Coming Church*, Edinburgh, Oliver and Boyd, 1967.

Schmaus, Michael, *Dogma*, 5 vols., Kansas City, Sheed & Ward, 1968.

Schroeder, H.J., O.P., *Canons and Decrees of the Council of Trent*, St. Louis, B. Herder Book Co., 1960.

SEDOS, eds., *Foundations of Mission Theology*, translated by John Drury, Maryknoll, New York, Orbis Books, 1972.

Segundo, Juan Luis, S.J., *Grace and the Human Condition*, Vol. II, *A Theology For Artisans of a New Humanity*. Translated by John Drury, Maryknoll, New York, Orbis Books, 1973.

——————., *The Community Called Church*, Vol. 1, *A Theology For Artisans of a New Humanity*. Translated by John Drury, Maryknoll, New York, Orbis Books, 1973.

Shea, John Gilmary, *The History of the Catholic Church in the United States*, 4 vols., New York, John G. Shea, n.d.

Shook, L.K., ed., *Renewal of Religious Thought. Proceedings of the Congress on the Theology of the Renewal of the Church Centenary of Canada, 1867-1967*, Vol. 1 with an Introduction by Paul-Emile Cardinal Léger, Vol. II with an Introduction by Leon-Joseph Cardinal Suenens, New York, Herder & Herder, 1968.

Structures Sociales et Pastorale Paroissiale, (Cangrès National de Lille, 1948), Paris, Union des Oeuvres Catholiques de France.

Suhard, Emmanuel Cardinal, *Growth or Decline? The Church Today*, translated by James A. Corbett, South Bend, Indiana, Fides Publishers, 1948.

Swanston, Hamish, F.G., *The Community Witness: An Exploration of Some of the Influences at Work in the New Testament Community and its Writings*, New York, Sheed & Ward, 1967.

Sweet, William Warren, *The Story of Religion in America*, New York, Harper & Bros., 1939.

Tyrrell, Francis M., *Man: Believer and Unbeliever,* New York, Alba House, 1974.

Underhill, Evelyn, *Worship,* New York, Harper & Bros., 1937.

Vagaggini, Cyprian, O.S.B., *Theological Dimensions of the Liturgy,* translated by Leonard J. Doyle, Collegeville, Minnesota, The Liturgical Press, 1959.

Van Noort, Monsignor G., *Dogmatic Theology,* Vol. I, *The True Religion,* From the Fifth Edition, Edited by Rev. J.P. Verhaar, translated and revised by John J. Castelot and William R. Murphy, Westminster, Maryland, The Newman Press, 1961.

von Allmen, J.-J., *Worship: Its Theology and Practice,* New York, Oxford University Press, 1965.

Ward, Leo R., C.S.C., *The Living Parish,* Notre Dame, Fides Publishers Association, 1959.

Winter, Michael M., *Blueprint for a Working Church: A Study in New Pastoral Structures,* St. Meinrad, Indiana, Abbey Press, 1973.

Witnessing to the Kingdom in a Dehumanizing World, Canadian Religious Conference, 1975, Ottawa, Ontario, "Donum Dei" Series, No. 22.

Woywood, Stanislaus, O.F.M., *The New Canon Law: A Commentary and Summary of the New Code of Canon Law,* with a Preface by Right Rev. Msgr. Philip Bernardini, New York, Joseph F. Wagner (Inc.), 1918.

Zehnle, Richard, *The Making of the Christian Church,* Notre Dame, Fides Publishers, Inc., 1969.

ARTICLES

Balasuriya, Tissa, "Rethinking the Church's Mission," *America*, (Sept. 9, 1972), pp. 144-147.

Barr, Browne, "Bury the Parish?", *The Christian Century*, 84, (Feb. 15, 1967), pp. 199-202.

Baum, Gregory, "Sociologists Look at Religion," *The Ecumenist* 11, (May-June, 1973), pp. 61-64.

————., "Tensions in the Catholic Church," *The Ecumenist* 7, (Jan.-Feb., 1969), pp. 21-26.

Bea, Augustine Cardinal, "The Eucharist and the Union of Christians," *Diakonia* I, (1966), pp. 242-255.

Bergmann, Michel, "Structures de l'Eglise pour aujourd'hui," *Verbum Caro* XVII, pp. 39-50.

Boitel, Philippe, "Quelles églises pour demain?", *Informations Catholiques internationales*, (July 15, 1971).

Braaten, Carl E., "The Church in Ecumenical and Cultural Cross-Fire," *Theology Digest* XV, (Winter, 1967), pp. 285-294.

Brown, Robert McAfee, "Ecumenism and the Secular Order," *Theology Digest* XV, (1967), pp. 259-271.

Browne, Henry J., "Groping for Relevance in an Urban Parish, St. Gregory the Great, New York City," *Cross Currents*, (Fall, 1971), pp. 433ff.

Bryant, M. Darrol, "Beyond Messianism, Toward a New 'American' Civil Religion," *The Ecumenist* 11, (May-June, 1973), pp. 49-51.

Chenu, M.D., "Toward Constitutional Development in the Church," *Information and Documentation on the Conciliar Church* 69-1, (Jan. 7, 1968).

——————., "Vox Populi, Vox Dei. Public Opinion in the People of God," *Information and Documentation on the Conciliar Church* 67-67, (Dec. 10, 1967).

Colson, J., "Qu'est-ce qu'un diocèse?" *Nouvelle Revue Theologique* LXXV, (1953).

Congar, Yves, "L'influence de la société et de l'histoire," *Nouvelle Revue Théologique*, (Juillet-Aout, 1974), pp. 675-692.

Cooke, Bernard J., "Intercommunion With the Orthodox," *Diakonia* I, (1966), pp. 256-262.

Crichton, J.D., "The Parish," *Liturgy* XXIX, (1960), pp. 1-4; pp. 28-32; 53-60.

Daoust, J., "La paroisse après Vatican II," *Esprit et Vie* No. 50, (11 Decembre, 1975), pp. 724-726.

Davis, Charles, "The Parish and Theology," *The Clergy Review* XLIX, (May, 1964), pp. 265-290.

de Certeau, Michel, "How is Christianity Thinkable Today?" *Theology Digest* 19, (Winter, 1971), pp. 334-345.

DeWitt, John, "Making a Community out of a Parish," *Cross Currents*, (Spring, 1966), pp. 197-211.

DuBay, William H., "Democratic Structures in the Church," *Chicago Studies* 3, (Fall, 1964), pp. 133-152.

Dulles, Avery, "Current Trends in Mission Theology," *Theology Digest* 20, (Spring, 1972), pp. 26-34.

Fahey, Michael A., "Continuity in the Church Amid Structural Changes," *Theological Studies* 35, (March, 1974), pp. 415-440.

Feltin, Maurice Cardinal, "Quelques réflexions sur le paroisse," *La Maison-Dieu* IX, (1947), pp. 104-112.

Fichter, Joseph H., "The Open Church in an Open Society," *The Catholic World* 201, (April, 1967), pp. 16-21.

Filteau, Jerry, "Calls Ministry for Justice 'Center Stage' of Church," *The Michigan Catholic*, (Feb. 11, 1976), p. 5.

Fitzpatrick, Joseph P., "Parish of the Future," *America,* (Nov. 6, 1965), pp. 521-523.

Fransen, Piet, "Episcopal Conferences: Crucial Problem of the Council," *Cross Currents,* (Summer, 1963), pp. 349-371.

Gaffney, James, "The Secular City: Roszak's Demolition Plan," *America,* (Nov. 18, 1972), pp. 410-412.

Gallen, John, "American Liturgy: A Theological Locus," *Theological Studies* 35, (June, 1974), pp. 302-311.

Grasso, D., "Osservazioni sulla teologia della parrocchia," *Gregorianum,* (1959), pp. 293-314.

Greeley, Andrew M., "The New Community," *The Critic,* (June-July, 1966), pp. 32-37.

—————., "The Question of the Parish as a Community," *Worship* XXXVI, III, pp. 136-143.

Grootaers, J., "Structures and Living Communities in the Conciliar Church," *Information and Documentation on the Conciliar Church* 67-15/16, (May, 14, 1967).

Harmon, John J., "The Church in the City," *Cross Currents* 13, (Spring 1963), pp. 149-163.

—————., "The Parish: When Is It Alive?—When Should It Die?", *Cross Currents,* (Fall, 1965), pp. 385-392.

—————., "Toward a Theology of the City Church," *Cross Currents* XIV, (Fall, 1964), pp. 401-415.

Hebblethwaite, Peter, "The Church of the Future," *Commonweal,* (December 19, 1975), pp. 617-624.

Hennelly, Alfred T., "'Church and World' and Theological Developments," *America,* (Feb. 28, 1976), pp. 153-156.

Hoffman, Ronan, "Conversion and the Mission of the Church," *Journal of Ecumenical Studies* 5, (Winter, 1968), pp. 1-20.

Kilian, Sabbas J., "Authority in the Church," *Thought* 44, (1969), pp. 69-82.

—————., "Dialogue in Ecclesiology," *Theological Studies* 30, (March, 1969), pp. 61-78.

—————., "Fundamental Option: An Essential Datum

of the Human Person," *The American Benedictine Review* XXI 2, (June, 1970), pp. 192-202.

—————., "The Catholic Theologian and Non-Christian Religions," *Thought* 49, (March, 1974), pp. 21-42.

—————., "The Question of Authority in 'Humanae Vitae,'" *Thought* 44, (1969).

Lecuyer, Joseph, "The Liturgical Assembly: Biblical and Patristic Foundations," *Concilium*, Vol. 12, *The Church Worships*, New York, Paulist Press, 1966, pp. 3-18.

Légaut, Marcel, "A Glimpse at Tomorrow's Church," *Cross Currents* XXIII, (Spring, 1973), pp. 1-30.

Lemieux, Raymond. "The Church and the Survival of Canada," *The Ecumenist* 11, (May-June, 1973), pp. 56-60.

Mason, John Ramon, "'Toward an American Theology': An Appraisal," *The Ecumenist* 7, (Jan.-Feb., 1969), pp. 26-29.

May, John L., "Failure in Faith: Failure in Preaching?", *America*, (Aug. 19, 1972).

McGowan, Thomas, "American Theology," *Commonweal*, (June 30, 1972), pp. 353-356.

Mollard, George, "A Parish Priest," *Cross Currents* 12, (Spring, 1962), pp. 156-167.

Moran, Robert E., "Theology of the Parish," *Worship* XXXVIII, VII, pp. 421-426.

Murray, John Courtney, "The Issue of Church and State at Vatican Council II," *Theological Studies* 27, (1966), pp. 580-606.

Nabaa, Philip, "Ecumenism and Intercommunion According to Vatican II," *Diakonia* I, (1966), pp. 294-298.

O'Meara, Thomas, "Karl Rahner on Priest, Parish, and Deacon," *Worship* 40, pp. 103-110.

Panikkar, Raymond, "Christians and So-Called Non-Christians," *Cross Currents*, (Summer, 1972), pp. 281-308.

Pintard, J., "L'église locale comme lieu de divinisation," *Esprit et Vie,* No. 25, (24 Juin, 1971), pp. 385-394.

Rahner, Karl, "Christianity and the New Earth," *Theology Digest* XV, (Winter, 1967), pp. 275-282.

————————., "Is the Church Sent to Humanize the World?",
  Theology Digest 20, (Spring, 1972), pp. 18-23.

————————., "Should the Church Solve the World's Problems?", *Listening*, (Winter, 1967), pp. 4-17.

————————., "Structural Changes in the Church," *Theology Digest* 23, (1975), pp. 203-209.

Robinson, John, "Community, the Church and the Non-
  Church," *Cross Currents* 12, (Winter, 1967), pp. 1-5.

Rose, Stephen C., "The Grass Roots Church," *Christianity* &
  Crisis 26, (July 25, 1966), pp. 168-171.

Reuther, Rosemary, "Post-Ecumenical Christianity," *The
  Ecumenist* 5, (Nov.-Dec., 1966), pp. 3-7.

Schillebeeckx, E., "The Synod of Bishops: Crisis of Faith
  and Local Church," *Information and Documentation
  on the Conciliar Church* 67-24, (July 23, 1967).

Schurr, Maurice, "The Parish as a Supernatural Reality,"
  Orate Fratres 12, (1938), pp. 255-459.

Schuyler, Joseph B., "The Parish Frontier," *Catholic Mind*
  62, (Jan., 1964), pp. 51-55.

Scott, Marshal L., "The Christian Ministry in an Advanced
  Technological Age," *Union Seminary Quarterly Review*
  XXI, (May, 1966).

"Seminaries Unclear About Mission of Church," *The Michigan Catholic*, (Jan. 28, 1976), p. 5.

Spiaggi, R., "Spunti per una teologia della parrocchia,"
  La Scuola Cattolica 80, (1952), pp. 26-42.

Steeman, T., "Political Relevance of the Christian Community Between Integralism and Critical Commitment,"
  Concilium 84, (1973), pp. 40-47.

Sullivan, William J., "American Catholicism: Toward the
  Year 2000," *Theology Digest* 20, (Winter, 1972), pp.
  341-348.

Thorman, J., "Report on the Underground Church," *Catholic Mind* 65, (Oct., 1967), pp. 6-9.

van der Poel, Cornelius, "Common Participation in Worship,"
  Diakonia I, (1966), pp. 282-293.

Wintersig, Athanasius, "Le realisme mystique de la paroisse," *Le Maison-Dieu,* No. 8, (1936), pp. 15-27.

Wolvington, K.H., "Local Churches are as Irrelevant as Denominations," *Christianity & Crisis* 26, (July 25, 1966), pp. 176-178.

Wood, Geoffrey, "The Future of Catholic Christianity," *Cross Currents* 12, (Summer, 1967), pp. 257-269.

Zizioulas, John D., "Apostolic Continuity and Orthodox Theology: Towards a Synthesis of Two Perspectives," *St. Vladimir's Theological Quarterly* 19, (1975), pp. 75-108.

————————., "The Eucharistic Community and the Catholicity of the Church," *One in Christ* VI, (1970), pp. 314-337.